It's another Quality Book from CGP

This book is for anyone doing OCR Science — Staged Assessment.

Whatever subject you're doing it's the same
old story — there are lots of facts and you've just got
to learn them. OCR Science is no different.

Happily this CGP book gives you all that important
information as clearly and concisely as possible.

It's also got some daft bits in to try and make the whole
experience at least vaguely entertaining for you.

Some of the material is only needed at Higher level.
We've stuck this stuff in blue boxes (like this one) so it's easy to find in the book.

What CGP is all about

Our sole aim here at CGP is to produce the highest quality books
— carefully written, immaculately presented and dangerously
close to being funny.

Then we work our socks off to get them out to you
— at the cheapest possible prices.

Year 11 Revision Guide — Contents

Year 11 Revision Guide

Contents

Published by: Coordination Group Publications Ltd
Illustrations by: Sandy Gardner e-mail: illustrations@sandygardner.co.uk
                       and Bowser, Colorado USA

Updated by: Matthew Ball
                       Chris Bates
                       Gemma Hallam
                       Tim Major
                       Tessa Moulton
                       Andy Park
                       Philip Robson
                       Julie Schofield

ISBN 1 84146 951 3
Groovy Website: www.cgpbooks.co.uk

Printed by Elanders Hindson, Newcastle upon Tyne.
Clipart sources: CorelDRAW and VECTOR.

Variation

The word "variation" sounds far too fancy for its own good. All it means is how animals or plants of the same species look or behave slightly different from each other. You know, a bit taller or a bit fatter or a bit more scary-to-look-at etc.

There are two causes of variation: Genetic Variation and Environmental Variation. Read on, and learn...

1) Genetic Variation

1) All animals are bound to be slightly different from each other cos their genes are slightly different.
2) Genes are the code inside all your cells which determine how you turn out.
   We all end up with a slightly different set of genes.
3) The exceptions to that rule are identical twins, because their genes are exactly the same.
   But even identical twins are never completely identical — and that's because of the other factor:

2) Environmental Variation is shown up by Twins

If you're not sure what "environment" means, think of it as "upbringing" instead
— it's pretty much the same thing — how and where you were "brought up".

Since we know the twins' genes are identical, any differences between them
must be caused by slight differences in their environment throughout their lives.

Twins give us a fairly good idea of how important the two factors (genes and environment)
are, compared with each other, at least for animals — plants always show much greater
variation due to differences in their environment than animals do, as explained below.

3) Environmental Variation in Plants is much Greater

Plants are strongly affected by:

1) Temperature,   2) Sunlight,   3) Moisture level,   4) Soil composition.

For example, plants may grow twice as big or twice as fast due to fairly
modest changes in environment such as the amount of sunlight or rainfall
they're getting, or how warm it is or what the soil is like.

*A cat, on the other hand, born and bred in the North of Scotland, could be sent out to
live in equatorial Africa and would show no significant changes — it would look the same,
eat the same, and it would probably still puke up everywhere.*

Animal Characteristics NOT affected at all by Environment:

1) EYE COLOUR.
2) HAIR COLOUR in most animals (but not humans where vanity plays a big part).
3) INHERITED DISEASES like haemophilia, cystic fibrosis, etc.
4) BLOOD GROUP.   And that's about it! So learn those four in case they ask you.

4) Combinations of Genetic and Environmental Variation

Everything else is determined by a mixture of genetic and environmental factors:
Body weight, height, skin colour, condition of teeth, academic or athletic prowess, etc. etc.

The tricky bit is working out just how significant environmental factors are for all these other features.
It's not at all easy to tell how much of your health, athletic ability and (most importantly) personality is
due to genes and how much to upbringing (environment). It's quite a hot topic these days.

Don't let everything get to you — just learn the facts...

Imagine you got mixed up with another baby at the hospital and had grown up in a totally different
household from your own. How different would you be now? It's a big social issue, so it is.

Genes and Chromosomes

If you're going to get <u>anywhere</u> with this topic you definitely need to learn these confusing words and exactly what they mean. You have to <u>make sure you know</u> exactly what <u>DNA</u> is, what and where <u>chromosomes</u> are, and what and where a <u>gene</u> is. If you don't get that sorted out first, then anything else you read about them won't make a lot of sense to you — <u>will it</u>?

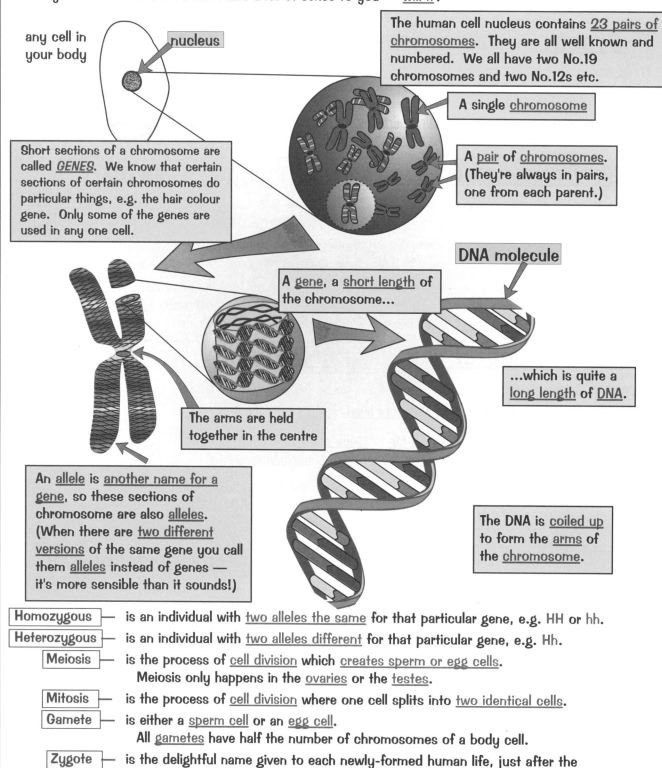

any cell in your body

nucleus

The human cell nucleus contains <u>23 pairs of chromosomes</u>. They are all well known and numbered. We all have two No.19 chromosomes and two No.12s etc.

A single <u>chromosome</u>

A <u>pair</u> of <u>chromosomes</u>. (They're always in pairs, one from each parent.)

Short sections of a chromosome are called <u>GENES</u>. We know that certain sections of certain chromosomes do particular things, e.g. the hair colour gene. Only some of the genes are used in any one cell.

DNA molecule

A <u>gene</u>, a <u>short length</u> of the chromosome...

...which is quite a <u>long length</u> of <u>DNA</u>.

The arms are held together in the centre

The DNA is <u>coiled up</u> to form the <u>arms</u> of the <u>chromosome</u>.

An <u>allele</u> is <u>another name for a</u> gene, so these sections of chromosome are also <u>alleles</u>. (When there are <u>two different versions</u> of the same gene you call them <u>alleles</u> instead of genes — it's more sensible than it sounds!)

Homozygous — is an individual with <u>two alleles the same</u> for that particular gene, e.g. HH or hh.

Heterozygous — is an individual with <u>two alleles different</u> for that particular gene, e.g. Hh.

Meiosis — is the process of <u>cell division</u> which <u>creates sperm or egg cells</u>.
Meiosis only happens in the <u>ovaries</u> or the <u>testes</u>.

Mitosis — is the process of <u>cell division</u> where one cell splits into <u>two identical cells</u>.

Gamete — is either a <u>sperm cell</u> or an <u>egg cell</u>.
All <u>gametes</u> have half the number of chromosomes of a body cell.

Zygote — is the delightful name given to each newly-formed human life, just after the (equally delightfully-named) *gametes* <u>fuse together</u> at fertilisation.

Hard to learn? — just try to get it straight...

This is a real easy page to learn, don't you think. Why, you could learn the whole thing with both ears tied behind your head. <u>Cover the page</u> and <u>scribble down</u> all the diagrams and details.

Mutations

A MUTATION occurs when an organism develops with some strange new characteristic that no other member of the species has had before. For example, if someone was born with blue hair it would be caused by a mutation. Some mutations are beneficial, but most are disastrous (eg blue hair).

Mutations are Caused by Faults in the DNA

There are several ways that mutations happen, but in the end they're all down to faulty DNA. Mutations usually happen when the DNA is replicating itself and something goes wrong.

1) Because DNA is what genes are made of, and also what chromosomes are made of, there are all these different definitions of what a mutation is:
   a) A mutation is faulty DNA, or a change in the DNA.
   b) A mutation is a change to a gene or several genes.
   c) A mutation is a change in the genetic code of one or more chromosomes.

2) A mutation starts in the nucleus of one particular cell.

3) A mutation happens when DNA isn't copied properly.

4) A mutation is caused by chemical changes in a gene, or in the DNA, or in a chromosome.

Radiation and Certain Chemicals cause Mutations

Mutations occur 'naturally', probably caused by "natural" background radiation (from the Sun, and rocks etc.) or just the laws of chance that every now and then the DNA doesn't quite copy itself properly. However the chance of mutation is increased by exposing yourself to:

1) Nuclear radiation, ie alpha, beta and gamma radiation. This is sometimes called ionising radiation because it creates ions (charged particles) as it passes through stuff. (See PD6.)

2) X-rays and Ultra-Violet light, which are the highest-frequency parts of the electromagnetic spectrum (together with gamma rays).

3) Certain chemicals which are known to cause mutations. Such chemicals are called mutagens. If the mutations produce cancer then the chemicals are often called carcinogens. Cigarette smoke contains chemical mutagens (or carcinogens)...

Most Mutations are Harmful

1) If a mutation occurs in reproductive cells, then the young may develop abnormally or die at an early stage of their development.

2) If a mutation occurs in body cells, the mutant cells may start to multiply in an uncontrolled way and invade other parts of the body. This is what we know as CANCER.

Some Mutations are Beneficial, giving us "EVOLUTION"

1) Blue "budgies" appeared suddenly as a mutation amongst yellow budgies. This is a good example of a neutral effect. It didn't harm its chances of survival and so it flourished (and at one stage, every grandma in Britain had one).

2) Very occasionally, a mutation will give the organism a survival advantage over its relatives. This is natural selection and evolution at work. A good example is a mutation in a bacterium that makes it resistant to antibiotics, so the mutant gene lives on, in the offspring, creating a resistant "strain" of bacteria.

Don't get your genes in a twist, this stuff's easy...

There are four sections with numbered points for each. Memorise the headings and learn the numbered points, then cover the page and scribble down everything you can remember. I know it makes your head hurt, but every time you try to remember the stuff, more of it sinks in. It'll all be worth it in the end.

Ordinary Cell Division: Mitosis

"Mitosis is when a cell reproduces itself ASEXUALLY by splitting to form two identical offspring that are called clones."

The really riveting part of the whole process is how the chromosomes split inside the cell. Learn and enjoy...

DNA all spread out in long strings.

DNA forms into chromosomes. Remember, the double arms are already duplicates of each other.

Chromosomes line up along the centre and then the cell fibres pull them apart, with the two halves of the chromosome going to opposite poles (ends) of the cell.

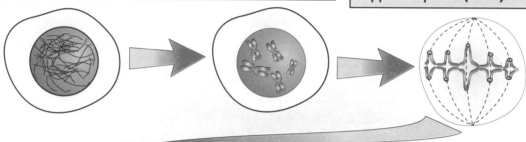

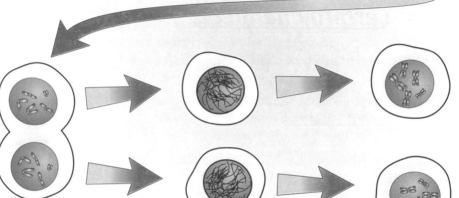

Membranes form around the two sets of chromosome threads. These become the nuclei of the two daughter cells.

The threads unwind into long strands of DNA and the whole process then starts over again.

(Note that the single chromosome threads have now duplicated themselves)

Mitosis and Asexual Reproduction

Mitosis produces new cells identical to the original cell. This is how all plants and animals grow and produce replacement cells. Cells throughout our body divide and multiply by this process. However some organisms also reproduce using this kind of cell division, bacteria being a good example. This is known as asexual reproduction. Here is a definition of it for you to learn:

> In asexual reproduction there is only one parent, and the offspring have exactly the same genes as the parent (ie: they're clones — see P.11).

This is because all the cells in both parent and offspring were produced by ordinary cell division, so they must all have identical genes in their cell nuclei. Asexual reproduction therefore produces no variation. Some plants reproduce asexually, eg potatoes, strawberries and daffodils (see P.11).

Now that I have your undivided attention...

You need to learn the definition of mitosis and the sequence of diagrams, and also the definition of asexual reproduction. Now cover the page and scribble down the two definitions and sketch out the sequence of diagrams — don't waste time with neatness — just find out if you've learnt it all yet.

Gamete Production: Meiosis

You thought mitosis was exciting. Hah! You ain't seen nothing yet. <u>Meiosis</u> is the other type of cell division. It only happens in the <u>reproductive organs</u> (ovaries and testes).

> <u>Meiosis</u> produces "<u>cells which have half the proper number of chromosomes</u>".
> Such cells are also known as "<u>haploid gametes</u>".

These cells are "genetically different" from each other because the genes all get <u>shuffled up</u> during meiosis and each gamete only gets <u>half</u> of them, selected at random.
Confused? I'm not surprised. But fear not, coz...   ....well worse things happen at sea...
The diagrams below will make it a lot clearer — but you have to <u>study</u> them pretty hard.

Reproductive cell in your testis or ovary.

1) Remember, in humans there are <u>23 pairs</u> of chromosomes at the start. That means 46 altogether, two of each type. In each <u>pair</u>, there is one you got from your <u>father</u>, and one you got from your <u>mother</u>.

They're called "<u>homologous pairs</u>" because <u>both</u> chromosomes have information about the <u>same aspects</u> of your body, e.g. hair colour, eye colour, etc., but one has information brought from your father (shown red) and one has information from your mother (shown blue). Note the little red y-chromosome.

2) The pairs now <u>split up</u> so that some of your father's chromosomes go with some of your mother's chromosomes, but there will be <u>no pairs</u> at all now. Just <u>one</u> of each of the 23 different types in each of the two new cells.
Each cell therefore has a <u>mixture</u> of your mother's and father's characteristics, but only has <u>half</u> the full complement of chromosomes.

3) These cells now split <u>mitosis-style</u>, with the chromosomes themselves splitting to form two identical cells, called <u>gametes</u>.
The twin-armed chromosomes were already duplicates, don't forget.

And that's meiosis done.
Note the difference between the first stage where the <u>pairs separate</u> and the second stage where the <u>chromosomes themselves split</u>. It's tricky!

<u>Gametes</u>
ie. sperm cells or egg cells.

Meiosis? Not even remotely scary...

There's a few tricky words in there which don't help — especially if you just ignore them...
The only way to <u>learn</u> this page is by constant reference to the diagram. Make sure you can sketch all the parts of it <u>from memory</u> and <u>scribble notes</u> to explain each stage. Even so, it's still difficult to understand it all, never mind remember it. But that's what you gotta do!

Module BD4 — Variation, Inheritance and Evolution   OCR Staged Assessment

Fertilisation: The Meeting of Gametes

There are 23 Pairs of Human Chromosomes

They are well known and numbered. In every cell nucleus we have two of each type. The diagram shows the 23 pairs of chromosomes from a human cell. One chromosome in each pair is inherited from each of our parents. Normal body cells have 46 chromosomes, in 23 homologous pairs.

Remember, "homologous" means that the two chromosomes in each pair are equivalent to each other. In other words, the number 19 chromosomes from both your parents pair off together, as do the number 17s etc. What you don't get is the number 12 chromosome from one parent pairing off with, say, the number 5 chromosome from the other.

Reproductive Cells undergo Meiosis to Produce Gametes:

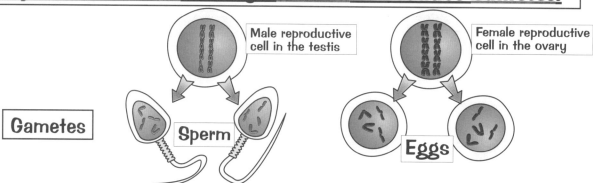

Male reproductive cell in the testis

Female reproductive cell in the ovary

Gametes

Sperm

Eggs

The gametes remember, only have one chromosome from each pair to describe each bit of you. The chromosome is picked randomly from the pair of chromosomes in the reproductive cell. This randomness leads to a unique individual with a unique mix of characteristics from both parents. But a normal cell needs two chromosomes of each type — one from each parent, so...

Fertilisation is the Joining Together of the Gametes

Here's a mouthful of a definition for you to learn:

> FERTILISATION is the fusion of haploid male and female gametes, restoring the diploid number of chromosomes in a zygote.

Put simply, fertilisation is when the sperm and the egg, with 23 chromosomes each, join together to form an offspring with a full 46 chromosomes. You've got to learn the posh definition though.

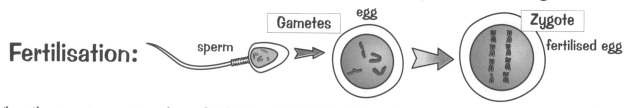

Fertilisation:

sperm

Gametes

egg

Zygote

fertilised egg

When the gametes meet up during fertilisation (FUSE), the 23 single chromosomes in one gamete will all pair off with their appropriate "partner chromosomes" from the other gamete to form the full 23 pairs again, No.4 with No.4, No.13 with No.13 etc. etc. Don't forget, the two chromosomes in a pair both contain the same basic genes, eg for hair colour, etc.

The resulting offspring will then receive its outward characteristics as a mixture from the two sets of chromosomes, so it will inherit features from both parents. Pretty cool, eh.

It should all be starting to come together now...

If you go through these last two pages you should see how the two processes, meiosis and fertilisation, are kind of opposite. Practise sketching out the sequence of diagrams, with notes, for both pages till it all sinks in. Nice, innit.

Monohybrid Crosses: Terminology

"Hey man, like *monohybrid crosses*, yeah right... ...so like, *what does it mean*, man?"   Just this, pal:

Breeding <u>two plants</u> or <u>animals</u>, who have <u>one gene different</u>, to see what you <u>get</u>.

It's always best done with a diagram like either of these:

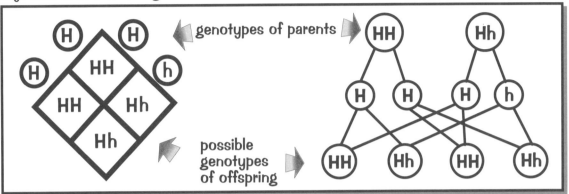

But first learn all these technical terms — it's real difficult to follow what's going on if you don't:

1) ALLELE

— this is just another name for a <u>gene</u>. If you have two <u>different versions</u> of a <u>gene</u>, like H and h, then you have to call them <u>alleles</u> instead of genes.

2) DOMINANT and RECESSIVE

— self explanatory. A dominant allele <u>dominates</u> a recessive allele.

3) GENOTYPE and PHENOTYPE

— <u>genotype</u> is just what '<u>type o' genes</u>' you've got, eg HH, Hh, or hh.
<u>Phenotype</u> sounds a lot like genotype but, irritatingly, is nothing like it at all.
Genotype is always a pair of letters like Hh, whilst <u>phenotype</u> is what <u>physical characteristics</u> result from the genotype, like "blue hair" or "big leaves" or "maleness".

4) "P1", "F1" and "F2" generations

The two <u>originals</u> that you cross are the <u>parental (P1) generation</u>, their <u>kids</u> are the <u>F1 generation</u> and the "<u>grandchildren</u>" are the <u>F2 generation</u>. Easy peasy.

5) HOMOZYGOUS and HETEROZYGOUS

— "Homo-" means "<u>same</u> kinda things", "Hetero-" means "<u>different</u> kinda things".
They stick "<u>-zygous</u>" on the end to show we're talking about <u>genes</u>, (rather than any other aspect of Biology), and also just to make it <u>sound more complicated</u>, I'm certain of it. So...

"<u>Homozygous recessive</u>" is the descriptive 'shorthand' (hah!) for this: hh
"<u>Homozygous dominant</u>" is the 'shorthand' for   HH
"<u>Heterozygous</u>" is the 'shorthand' for   Hh
"A <u>Homozygote</u>" or "a <u>Heterozygote</u>" are how you refer to people with such genes.

Let's try out the brilliant descriptive 'shorthand' shall we:

"Alexander is homozygous recessive for the baldness gene" is <u>so much easier</u> to say and understand than "Alex is bb".   Hmm, well, that's Biology for you.

Now it's time to homologate your intellectual stimuli...

You can't beat a fewdal big fancyfold wordsmiths to make things crystally clearasil, can you...
Anyway, half the Exam marks are for knowing the fancy words <u>so just keep learning 'em!</u>

Monohybrid Crosses: Hamsters

Cross-breeding Hamsters

It can be all too easy to find yourself cross-breeding hamsters, some with normal hair and a mild disposition and others with wild scratty hair and a leaning towards crazy acrobatics.

Let's say that the gene which causes the crazy nature is <u>recessive</u>, so we use a <u>small "h"</u> for it, whilst normal (boring) behaviour is due to a <u>dominant gene</u>, so we represent it with a <u>capital "H"</u>.
1) A <u>crazy hamster</u> must have the <u>genotype</u>: hh.
2) However, a <u>normal hamster</u> can have <u>two possible genotypes</u>:   HH or Hh.
  This is pretty important — it's the basic difference between dominant and recessive genes:

> To display <u>recessive characteristics</u> you must have
> <u>both alleles recessive</u>, hh, (ie be "homozygous recessive")
>
> But to display <u>dominant characteristics</u> you can be <u>either</u>
> HH ("homozygous dominant") or Hh ("heterozygous").

It's only that difference which makes monohybrid crosses even <u>remotely</u> interesting. If hh gave crazy hamsters, HH gave normal hamsters and Hh something in between, it'd all be pretty dull.

An Almost Unbearably Exciting Example

Let's take a thoroughbred crazy hamster, genotype hh, with a thoroughbred normal hamster, genotype HH, and cross breed them. You must learn this whole diagram thoroughly, till you can do it all yourself:

P1 Parents' <u>phenotype</u>:	Normal and boring	Wild and scratty
P1 Parents' <u>genotype</u>:	(HH)	(hh)
Gametes' <u>genotype</u>:	(H) (H)	(h) (h)
F1 Zygotes' <u>genotype</u>:	(Hh) (Hh)	(Hh) (Hh)
F1 Zygotes' <u>phenotype</u>:	They're all normal and boring	

<u>If two of these F1 generation now breed they will produce the F2 generation</u>:

F1 Parents' <u>phenotype</u>:	Normal and boring	Normal and boring
F1 Parents' <u>genotype</u>:	(Hh)	(Hh)
Gametes' <u>genotype</u>:	(H) (h)	(H) (h)
F2 Zygotes' <u>genotype</u>:	(HH) (Hh)	(hH) (hh)
F2 Zygotes' <u>phenotype</u>:	Normal Normal	Normal <u>Crazy!</u>

This gives a <u>3:1 ratio</u> of Normal to Crazy offspring in the F2 generation.
Remember that "<u>results</u>" like this are only <u>probabilities</u>. It doesn't mean it'll happen.
(Most likely, you'll end up trying to contain a mini-riot of nine lunatic baby hamsters.)

See how those fancy words start to roll off the tongue...

The diagram and all its fancy words need to be second nature to you. So practise writing it out <u>from memory</u> until you get it all right. Because when you can do one — <u>you can do 'em all</u>.

Girl or Boy? — X and Y Chromosomes

There are 23 matched pairs of chromosomes in every human cell.
You'll notice the 23rd pair are labelled XY. They're the two chromosomes
that decide whether you turn out <u>male or female</u>. They're called the X and
Y chromosomes because they look like an X and a Y.

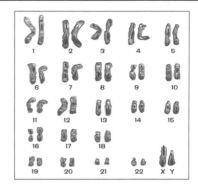

> <u>All men</u> have <u>an X</u> and <u>a Y</u> chromosome: XY
> <u>The Y chromosome is dominant</u> and causes <u>male characteristics</u>.
>
> <u>All women</u> have <u>two X chromosomes</u>: XX
> The XX combination allows <u>female characteristics</u> to develop.

The diagram below shows the way the male XY chromosomes and female XX chromosomes split up to
form the <u>gametes</u> (eggs or sperm), and then combine together at <u>fertilisation</u>.

The criss–cross lines show all the <u>possible</u> ways the X and Y chromosomes <u>could</u> combine.
Remember, <u>only one of these</u> would actually happen for any offspring.
What the diagram shows us is the <u>relative probability</u> of each type of zygote (offspring) occurring.

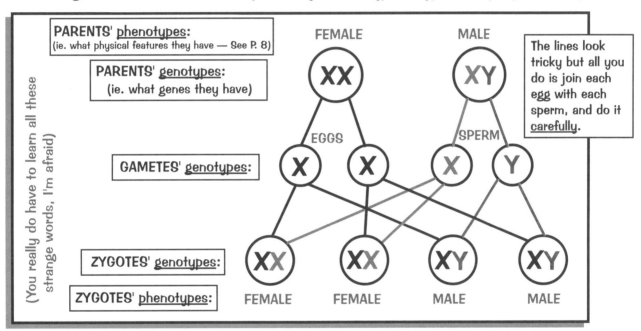

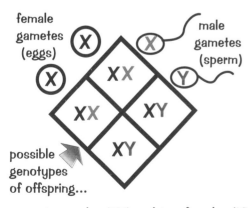

female gametes (eggs)

male gametes (sperm)

possible genotypes of offspring...

...two males (XY) and two females (XX).

The other way of doing this is with a <u>checkerboard</u>
type diagram. If you don't understand how it works, ask
"Teach" to explain it. The <u>pairs of letters</u> in the middle
show the <u>genotypes</u> of the possible offspring.

Both diagrams show that there'll be the same
proportion of male and female offspring, because there
are <u>two XX results</u> and <u>two XY results</u>.

Don't forget that this <u>50:50 ratio</u> is only a <u>probability</u>.
If you had four kids they <u>could</u> all be <u>boys</u> — yes I
know, terrifying isn't it.

How can it take all that just to say it's a 50:50 chance...

Make sure you know all about X and Y chromosomes and who has what combination.
The diagrams are real important. Practise reproducing them until you can do it <u>effortlessly</u>.

Genetic and Infectious Diseases

Diseases can be <u>inherited</u> through faulty genes, or caused by <u>infection</u>.

Cystic Fibrosis _is Caused by a_ Recessive Gene (Allele)

1) <u>Cystic Fibrosis</u> is a <u>genetic disease</u> which affects about <u>1 in 1600 people</u> in the UK.
2) The disorder cannot develop in a child unless both parents have the defective gene (ie. are carriers). There is still only a 1 in 4 chance that it <u>will</u> occur. A carrier has the <u>defective gene</u> without actually having the <u>disorder</u>.
3) It's a disorder of the <u>cell membranes</u> caused by a <u>defective gene</u>. The result of the <u>defective gene</u> is that the body produces a lot of thick sticky mucus in the lungs, which has to be removed by <u>massage</u>.
4) The <u>blockage of the air passages</u> in the lungs causes a lot of <u>chest infections</u>.
5) <u>Physiotherapy and antibiotics</u> clear them up but slowly the sufferer becomes more and more ill. There's still <u>no cure</u> or effective treatment for this condition.

The <u>genetics</u> behind cystic fibrosis is actually very straightforward. The gene which causes cystic fibrosis is a <u>recessive gene</u>, c, carried by about <u>1 person in 20</u>. The usual genetic inheritance diagram illustrates what goes on:

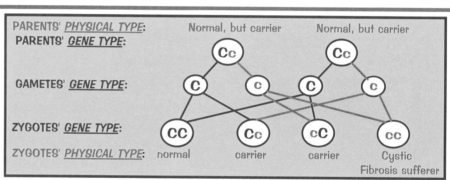

This diagram illustrates the <u>1 in 4 chance</u> of a child having the disease, if <u>both parents</u> are carriers.

Sickle Cell Anaemia — _Caused by a_ Recessive Allele

1) This disease causes the <u>red blood cells</u> to be shaped like <u>sickles</u> instead of the normal round shape. They then get <u>stuck</u> in the capillaries which <u>deprives body cells of oxygen</u>.

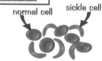

2) Parents may be <u>carriers</u> without showing the <u>symptoms</u>, but both parents must have the <u>defective gene</u> for the disease to appear in any of their children.
3) Even though sufferers may die <u>before they can reproduce</u>, the occurrence of sickle cell anaemia <u>doesn't always die out</u> as you'd expect it to, especially not in <u>Africa</u>.
4) This is because <u>carriers</u> of the recessive allele which causes it <u>are more immune to malaria</u>. Hence, being a carrier <u>increases</u> their chance of survival in some parts of the world, even though some of their offspring are going to die young from sickle cell anaemia.
5) The genetics are <u>identical</u> to <u>Cystic Fibrosis</u> because both diseases are caused by a <u>recessive allele</u>. Hence if <u>both</u> parents are carriers there's a <u>1 in 4 chance</u> each child will develop it.

Infectious Diseases — AIDS _is now the Most Serious_

<u>Infection</u> is the other main cause of disease. This can be from <u>bacteria or viruses</u>.

1) AIDS (Acquired Immunodeficiency Syndrome) is caused by a virus called <u>HIV</u>.
2) The virus is passed from one person to another in bodily fluids such as <u>blood</u> and <u>semen</u>. It doesn't live for long outside the body. That makes it a very <u>difficult</u> disease to catch.
3) There is, as yet, no successful <u>cure</u> for AIDS. The search continues for a <u>vaccine</u> against HIV.
4) Other viruses, like the <u>common cold</u>, <u>flu</u>, and <u>meningitis</u>, are far easier to catch, since the virus can be carried in the <u>air</u> (for a short time).

Learn the facts then see what you know...

These diseases are all mentioned in the <u>syllabus</u> and questions on them are <u>very likely</u>.
You need to <u>learn</u> all this very basic information on all three. <u>Cover the page</u> and <u>scribble</u> it all down.

Cloned Plants

Many Plants Produce Clones — all by themselves

This means they produce <u>exact genetic copies</u> of themselves <u>without involving another plant</u>.
Here are three common ones:

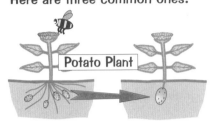 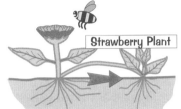 

1) New <u>potato plants</u> growing from tubers of old plant.

2) <u>Strawberry plants</u> producing <u>runners</u>. <u>Spider plants</u> can reproduce in the same way.

3) <u>Bulbs</u> such as <u>daffodils</u> growing new bulbs off the side of them.

Gardeners Make Clones from Cuttings

1) Gardeners are familiar with taking <u>cuttings</u> from good parent plants, and then planting them to produce <u>identical copies</u> (clones) of the parent plant.
2) The cuttings are kept in a <u>damp atmosphere</u> until their <u>roots develop</u>.
3) These plants can be produced <u>quickly and cheaply</u>.
4) These days, this basic technique has been given the <u>full high-tech treatment</u> by <u>commercial plant breeders</u>:

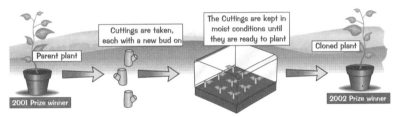

The Essentials of Commercial Cloning:

TISSUE CULTURE

This is where, instead of starting with at least a stem and bud, they just put <u>a few plant cells</u> in a <u>growth medium</u> containing <u>hormones</u> and it grows into <u>a new plant</u>. Just like that! Phew.

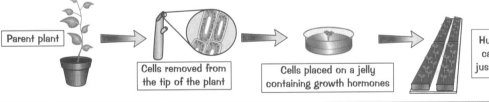

ADVANTAGES OF TISSUE CULTURE:

1) Very <u>fast</u> — can produce thousands of plantlets in a few weeks.
2) Very little <u>space</u> needed.
3) <u>Can grow all year</u> — no problem with weather or seasons.
4) New plants are <u>disease-free</u>.
5) All the <u>characteristics</u> of the plant are known.
6) <u>New plants</u> can be <u>developed</u> (quickly) by splicing new genes into plantlets and seeing how they turn out.

DISADVANTAGES OF TISSUE CULTURE:

The usual drawback with clones — <u>a reduced "gene pool"</u> leading to <u>vulnerability to new diseases</u> (see page 13). There is also the <u>ethical dilemma</u> in 'playing God'.

Stop cloning around — just learn it...

They could easily test your knowledge of <u>any</u> sentence on this page. I only put in stuff you need to know, you know. Practise scribbling out all the facts on this page, <u>mini-essay</u> style.

Selective Breeding

Selective Breeding is Very Simple

Selective breeding is also called artificial selection, because humans artificially select the plants or animals that are going to breed and flourish, according to what we want from them.
This is the basic process involved in selective breeding:

1) From your existing stock select the ones which have the best characteristics.

2) Breed them with each other.

3) Select the best of the offspring, and combine them with the best that you already have and breed again.

4) Continue this process over several generations to develop the desired traits.

Selective Breeding is Very Useful in Farming

Artificial selection like this is used in most areas of modern farming, to great benefit:

1) Better beef

Selectively breeding beef cattle to get the best beef (taste, texture, appearance, etc).

2) Better milk

Selectively breeding milking cows to increase milk yield and resistance to disease.

3) Better chickens

Selectively breeding chickens to improve egg size and number of eggs per hen.

4) Better wheat

Selectively breeding wheat to produce new varieties with better yields and better disease-resistance too.

5) Better flowers

Selectively breeding flowers to produce bigger and better and more colourful ones.

Selective Breeding

Selective breeding is all very well, but there are one or two problems associated with it.

The Main Drawback is a Reduction in the Gene Pool

In farming, animals are selectively bred to develop the best features, which are basically:

A) <u>Maximum Yield</u> of meat, milk, grain etc.

B) <u>Good Health</u> and <u>Disease Resistance</u>.

1) But selective breeding reduces the <u>number of alleles</u> in a population because the farmer keeps breeding from the "best" animals or plants — the same ones all the time.

Oh Eck!

2) This can cause serious problems if a <u>new disease appears</u>, as all the plants or animals could be wiped out.

3) This is made more likely because all the stock are <u>closely related</u> to each other, so if one of them is going to be killed by a new disease, the others are also likely to succumb to it.

| Selective Breeding | | Reduction in the number of different alleles (genes) | | Less chance of any resistant alleles being present in the population | Nothing to selectively breed a new strain from |

Selective Breeding in Pedigree Dogs Causes Bad Health

Most of the above <u>doesn't apply</u> to selective breeding in <u>pedigree dogs</u>, where <u>physical appearance</u> is the <u>only thing</u> that seems to matter — purely for winning dog shows. Selective breeding programmes can lead to accumulation of harmful recessive characteristics. Many pedigree dogs (in fact <u>most</u> pedigree dogs) have quite bad <u>health problems</u> because of this artificial selection.

Random Cross-Breeds Can be Much Healthier Dogs

1) Mongrels (random cross-breeds) on the other hand, are usually much <u>healthier</u>, <u>fitter</u> dogs because they're not so <u>interbred</u>.

2) They're very often much nicer natured and they can be real pretty too.

3) The word "<u>mongrel</u>" does them no justice at all. If you want a really great dog, my advice is go to the dog rescue place and get a crazy cross-breed and just love him.

Don't sit there brooding over it, just learn the info...

<u>Selective breeding is a very simple topic.</u> In the Exam they'll likely give you half a page explaining how a farmer in Sussex did this or that with his crops or cows, and then they'll suddenly ask: "<u>What is meant by selective breeding?</u>" That's when you just write down the four points at the top of page 12. Then they'll ask you to "<u>Suggest other ways that selective breeding might be used by farmers in Sussex to improve their yield</u>". That's when you just list some of the examples that you've learnt. They do like padding the questions out, don't they! In Olden Times (the 1970s) they would just have said: "<u>Explain what selective breeding is and give four examples of where it is used. — 8 Marks</u>" (!)

Genetic Engineering

Genetic engineering is a new science with exciting possibilities, but dangers, too.

Genetic Engineering is Ace — hopefully

The basic idea of genetic engineering is to move sections of <u>DNA</u> (genes) from one organism to another so that it produces <u>useful biological products</u>.

1) Crops such as <u>wheat</u> are <u>genetically modified</u> to be <u>resistant to weedkillers</u>.
   The farmer can spray the <u>whole field</u> with weedkiller and <u>only kill</u> the <u>weeds</u>.

2) Other food crops are genetically modified to be better for consumers. <u>Tomatoes</u> are genetically modified so that they <u>ripen more slowly</u>. This makes them <u>taste better</u> and go off less quickly.

3) Bacteria are used to produce <u>human insulin</u> for diabetes sufferers and also to produce <u>human growth hormone</u> for children who aren't growing properly.

Genetic Engineering involves these Important Stages:

1) The useful gene is "<u>cut</u>" from the DNA of, say, a human.

2) This is done using <u>enzymes</u>. Particular enzymes will cut out particular bits of DNA.

3) <u>Enzymes</u> are then used to <u>cut the DNA</u> of a <u>bacterium</u> and the human gene is then inserted.

4) Again this "<u>splicing</u>" of a new gene is controlled by certain <u>specific enzymes</u>.

5) The bacterium is now <u>cultivated</u> and soon there are <u>millions</u> of similar bacteria all producing, say, human insulin.

6) This can be done on an <u>industrial scale</u> and the useful product can be <u>separated out</u>.

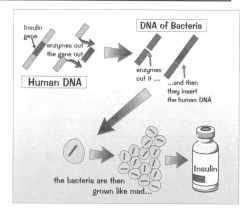

7) The same approach can also be used to <u>transfer useful genes into animal embryos</u>. Sheep for example can be developed which produce useful substances (ie. drugs) in <u>their milk</u>! This is a very easy way to produce drugs...

Genetic Engineering — Benefits and Problems

<u>Genetic engineering</u> of <u>crops</u> could make it possible to grow them in places they wouldn't grow before — good news for countries with lousy climates. Crops could also be genetically engineered to be more nutritious — preventing <u>malnutrition</u>.

Engineering weedkiller-resistant crops is a great way of <u>increasing yields</u>, but there are potential problems. Some people worry that farmers should be spraying <u>less</u> weedkiller on the land not more.

Genetic engineering of <u>humans</u> is currently restricted to <u>gene therapy</u> for diseases like cystic fibrosis that are caused by <u>faulty genes</u>. This means introducing <u>healthy</u> copies of the gene into the body of a person with the disease. Their <u>cells</u> will then be able to make the protein they need.

Genetic engineering of <u>sperm</u> and <u>egg</u> cells would allow genetic diseases to be eliminated in <u>future generations</u>. It could also be used to create '<u>designer babies</u>' with only the genetic traits preferred by their parents. A lot of people are strongly <u>against</u> this.

There's also a possibility that any inserted genes might have unexpected harmful effects.

Now I'm ready to create my monster...

Genetic engineering — it's a bit like my cat. Except it doesn't pounce on things. And it doesn't eat loads. And you can't stroke it. And it doesn't purr. And it can't miaow. And it doesn't...

Fossils and Evolution

The Theory of Evolution is Cool

1) This suggests that all the animals and plants on Earth gradually "evolved" over millions of years, rather than just suddenly popping into existence. Makes sense.

2) Life on Earth began as simple organisms living in water and gradually everything else evolved from there. And it only took about 3,000,000,000 years.

Fossils Provide Evidence for it

1) Fossils provide lots of evidence for evolution — they're the "remains" of plants and animals which lived millions of years ago.

2) They show how today's species have changed and developed over millions of years.

3) There are quite a few "missing links" though because the fossil record is incomplete. This is because very very few dead plants or animals actually turn into fossils. There are also fossils yet to be discovered that might help complete the picture.

4) Hundreds of years ago, people didn't realise that fossils were evidence of evolution. They thought fossils were just quirks of the rock. When people realised that fossils were the remains of living creatures, they preferred to think that they were of animals that were still around, but hadn't been discovered yet. People's religious beliefs made it difficult for them to think that species could be made extinct, or that species could change over time.

There are Three ways that Fossils can be Formed:

1) FROM THE HARD PARTS OF ANIMALS   (Most fossils happen this way.)

Things like bones, teeth, shells, etc, which don't decay easily, can last a long time when buried. They're eventually replaced by minerals as they decay, forming a rock-like substance shaped like the original hard part. The surrounding sediments also turn to rock, but the fossil stays distinct inside the rock, until someone digs it up.

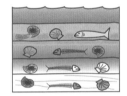

2) FROM THE SOFTER PARTS OF ANIMALS OR PLANTS — PETRIFICATION

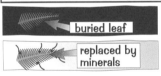

buried leaf

replaced by minerals

Sometimes fossils are formed from the softer parts which somehow haven't decayed. The soft material gradually becomes "petrified" (turns to stone) as it slowly decays and is replaced by minerals. This is rare, since there are very few occasions when decay occurs so slowly.

3) IN PLACES WHERE NO DECAY HAPPENS

a) INSECTS are often found fully preserved in AMBER — FOSSILISED RESIN. There's no OXYGEN or MOISTURE in the amber so decay microbes can't survive.

b) IN GLACIERS it's too COLD for the decay microbes to work. A HAIRY MAMMOTH was found fully preserved in a glacier somewhere several years

c) WATERLOGGED BOGS are too ACIDIC for decay microbes. A 10,000 year old man was found in a bog a few years ago. He was dead, and a bit squashed but otherwise well preserved, although it was clear he'd been murdered.

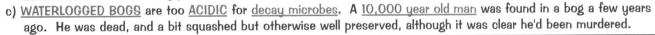

Extinction is Pretty Bad News

The dinosaurs became EXTINCT and it's only FOSSILS that tell us they ever existed at all.

There are THREE WAYS a species can become EXTINCT:
1) The ENVIRONMENT CHANGES too quickly.
2) A new PREDATOR or DISEASE kills them all.
3) They can't COMPETE with another (new) species for FOOD.

As the environment changes, some plant and animal species evolve and survive.
Many species, however, can't cope and may be wiped out, ie. extinction.

Don't get bogged down in all this information...

Make sure you're fully aware of the three different types of fossil and how they're formed.
Also make sure that you know the factors that cause extinction. Learn, cover and scribble...

Natural Selection

Charles Darwin's Theory of Natural Selection is Ace

1) This theory is cool and provides a comprehensive explanation for all life on Earth.

2) Mind you, it caused some trouble at the time, because for the first time ever, there was a highly plausible explanation for our own existence, without the need for a "Creator".

3) This was bad news for the religious authorities of the time, who tried to ridicule old Charlie's ideas. But, as they say, "the truth will out".

Darwin made Four Important Observations...

1) All organisms produce more offspring than could possibly survive.

2) But in fact, population numbers tend to remain fairly constant over long periods of time.

3) Organisms in a species show wide variation due to different genes.

4) Some of the variations are inherited and passed on to the next generation.

...and then made these Two Deductions:

1) Since most offspring don't survive, all organisms must have to struggle for survival.
   (Being eaten, disease and competition cause large numbers of individuals to die.)

2) The ones who survive and reproduce will pass on their genes.

This is the famous "Survival of the fittest" statement. Organisms with slightly less survival value will probably perish first, leaving the strongest and fittest to pass on their genes to the next generation.

Mutations play a big part in Natural Selection...

...by creating a new feature with a high survival value. Once upon a time maybe all rabbits had short ears and managed OK. Then one day out popped a mutant with big ears who was always the first to dive for cover. Pretty soon he's got a whole family of them with big ears, all diving for cover before the other rabbits, and before you know it there're only big-eared rabbits left because the rest just didn't hear trouble coming quick enough.

(Eat your heart out, Rudyard Kipling)

FOX!

Most mutations are harmful (see P. 3), but some are beneficial. Beneficial mutations make natural selection work.

All Wild Creatures live in a very Harsh World indeed...

The natural world may seem like a paradise on Earth to a lot of people, but the reality for the wild creatures that live in it is quite different.

The natural world is in fact a very harsh environment where many offspring die young, due to predators, disease and competition.

But remember, this is an important element in the process of natural selection. There has to be a large surplus of offspring for nature to select the fittest from.

Life for any farm animal is a veritable dream compared to the "eat or be eaten" savage reality of the 'natural' world. Most wild animals are eventually either eaten alive or else they starve to death. Think about it — they've all gotta go somehow. Give them a nice cosy civilised farm any day, I say...

"Natural Selection" — sounds like Vegan Chocolates...

This page is split into five sections. Memorise the headings, then cover the page and scribble down all you can about each section. Keep trying until you can remember all the important points.

Revision Summary for Module BD4

Gee, all that business about genes and chromosomes and the like — it's all pretty serious stuff, don't you think? It takes a real effort to get your head round it all. There's too many big fancy words, for one thing. But there you go — life's tough and you've just gotta face up to it. Use these questions to find out what you know — and what you don't. Then look back and learn the bits you didn't know. Then try the questions again, and again...

1) What are the two types of variation? Describe their relative importance for plants and animals.

2) List four features of animals which aren't affected at all by environment, and four which are.

3) Draw a set of diagrams showing the relationship between: cell, nucleus, chromosomes, genes, DNA.

4) Give three definitions of what a mutation is. List the three main causes of mutations.

5) Give an example of harmful, neutral and beneficial mutations.

6) Give a definition of mitosis. Draw a set of diagrams showing what happens in mitosis.

7) What is asexual reproduction? Give a proper definition for it. How does it involve mitosis?

8) Where does meiosis take place? What kind of cells does meiosis produce?

9) Draw out the sequence of diagrams showing what happens during meiosis.

10) How many pairs of chromosomes are there in a normal human cell nucleus?

11) What happens to the chromosome numbers during meiosis and then during fertilisation?

12) Give three different examples of plants cloning themselves in nature.

13) Write down the methods, advantages and disadvantages of commercial plant cloning and tissue culture.

14) What is meant by monohybrid crosses?

15) Define the words 'genotype' and 'phenotype'. Use examples.

16) Give three examples of the wonderful genetics descriptive shorthand.

17) Starting with parental genotypes HH and hh, draw a full genetic inheritance diagram to show the eventual genotypes and phenotypes of the F1 and F2 generations (of hamsters).

18) What are X and Y chromosomes to do with? Who has what combination?

19) Draw a genetic inheritance diagram to show how these genes are passed on.

20) What are the two main ways that disease is caused? Give an example of each.

21) List the symptoms and treatment of cystic fibrosis. What causes this disease?

22) Draw a genetics diagram to show the probability of a child being a sufferer.

23) Give the cause and symptoms of sickle cell anaemia. Why does it not die out?

24) Describe the basic procedure in selective breeding (of cows).

25) What is the main drawback of selective breeding in pedigree dogs?

26) Using diagrams, describe the process of genetic engineering.
Give an important use of genetic engineering in industry.

27) Why is the fossil record incomplete?

28) Describe fully the three ways that fossils can form. Give examples of each type.

29) What are the three main factors that cause extinction?

30) What were Darwin's four observations and two deductions?

31) Explain how mutation and a harsh environment play a big part in natural selection.

Basic Plant Structure

You have to know all these parts of a plant and what they do:

The Five Different Bits of a Plant all do Different Jobs

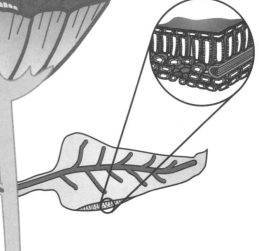

1) Flower

THIS ATTRACTS INSECTS such as bees which carry pollen between different plants. This allows the plants to be pollinated so they can reproduce.

2) Leaf

It produces FOOD for the plant. I'll say it again, listen....
THE LEAF PRODUCES ALL THE FOOD THAT THE PLANT NEEDS.

Plants do not take food from the soil.
Plants make all their own food in their leaves using PHOTOSYNTHESIS.

(That's a bit of a shocker when you think about it. Imagine making all your own food under your skin just by lying in the sun — and never having to eat at all!)

3) Stem

1) This holds the plant UPRIGHT.
2) Also, WATER and FOOD travel up and down the stem.

4) Root hairs

These give A BIG SURFACE AREA to absorb water and mineral ions from the soil.

5) Root

1) Its main job is ANCHORAGE.
2) It also takes in water and a few mineral ions from the soil. But mostly just water.
REMEMBER, plants do NOT take "food" in from the soil.

The Big Idea is to LEARN all that...

Everything on this page is there to be LEARNT because it's very likely to come up in your Exams.
This is pretty basic stuff, but it can still catch you out if you don't learn it properly.
For example: "What is the main function of the root?". Too many people answer "Taking food from the soil" — Eeek! LEARN these facts. They all count. They're all worth marks in the Exam. Practise until you can sketch the diagram and scribble down ALL the details, without looking back.

Diffusion

Don't be put off by the fancy word

"Diffusion" is really simple. It's just the <u>gradual movement of particles</u> from <u>places where there are lots of them</u> to places where there are <u>less of them</u>.

That's all it is — <u>IT'S JUST THE NATURAL TENDENCY FOR STUFF TO SPREAD OUT</u>.

Unfortunately you also have to <u>LEARN</u> the fancy way of saying the same thing, which is this:

DIFFUSION is the <u>MOVEMENT OF PARTICLES</u> from an area of <u>HIGH CONCENTRATION</u> to an area of <u>LOW CONCENTRATION</u>

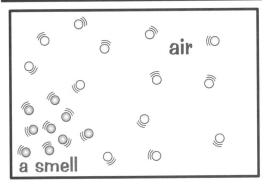
air

a smell

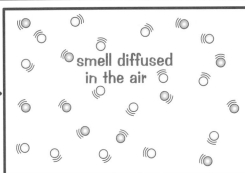
smell diffused in the air

Diffusion of <u>Gases in Leaves</u> is vital for <u>Photosynthesis</u>

The <u>simplest type</u> of diffusion is where <u>different gases diffuse through each other</u>, like when a weird smell spreads out through the air in a room. Diffusion of gases also happens in <u>leaves</u> and they'll very likely put it in your Exam. <u>So learn it now</u>:

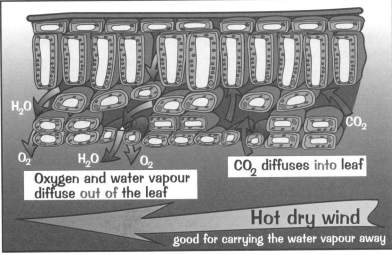
H_2O
O_2 H_2O O_2

Oxygen and water vapour diffuse out of the leaf

CO_2 diffuses into leaf

CO_2

Hot dry wind
good for carrying the water vapour away

For <u>PHOTOSYNTHESIS</u> to happen, <u>carbon dioxide</u> gas has to get <u>inside the leaves</u>.

It does this by <u>DIFFUSION</u> through the biddy little holes under the leaf called <u>stomata</u>. (One <u>stoma</u>, two <u>stomata</u>.)

At the same time <u>water vapour</u> and <u>oxygen</u> diffuse <u>out</u> through the same biddy little holes.

The water vapour escapes by <u>diffusion</u> because <u>there's a lot of it inside the leaf</u> and <u>less of it in the air outside</u>. <u>This diffusion causes TRANSPIRATION</u> (see P22) <u>and it goes quicker</u> when the air around the leaf is kept <u>DRY</u> — ie. transpiration is quickest in <u>HOT, DRY, WINDY CONDITIONS</u> — and don't you forget it!

So, how much do you know about diffusion?

Yeah sure it's a pretty book but actually the big idea is to <u>learn</u> all the stuff that's in it.

So learn this page until you can answer these questions <u>without having to look back</u>:

1) Write down the definition for diffusion, and then say what it means in your own words.
2) Draw the cross-section of the leaf with arrows to show which way the three gases diffuse.
3) What weather conditions make the diffusion of water vapour out of the leaf go fastest?

Diffusion Through Cell Membranes

Cell membranes are kind of clever...

They're kind of clever because they hold everything <u>inside</u> the cell, <u>BUT</u>, they let stuff <u>in and out</u> as well. Only very <u>small molecules</u> can diffuse through cell membranes though — things like <u>glucose</u> or <u>amino acids</u>.

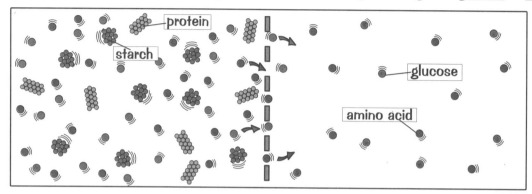

1) Notice that <u>BIG MOLECULES</u> like <u>STARCH</u> or <u>PROTEINS</u> can't diffuse through cell membranes — they could quite cheerfully ask you exactly that in the Exam.
2) Just like with diffusion in air, particles flow through the cell membrane from where there's a <u>HIGH CONCENTRATION</u> (a lot of them) to where there's a <u>LOW CONCENTRATION</u> (not such a lot of them).

Osmosis is a Special Case of Diffusion, that's all

> **OSMOSIS** is the *movement of water molecules* across a *partially permeable membrane* from a region of **HIGH WATER CONCENTRATION** to a region of **LOW WATER CONCENTRATION**.

1) A <u>partially permeable membrane</u> is just one with <u>real small holes</u> in it. So small, in fact, that <u>only water molecules</u> can pass through them, and bigger molecules like <u>glucose</u> can't.
2) <u>Visking tubing</u> is a partially permeable membrane that you should learn the <u>name</u> of. It's also called <u>dialysis tubing</u> because it's used in <u>kidney dialysis machines</u>.
3) The water molecules actually pass <u>both ways</u> through the membrane in a <u>two-way traffic</u>.
4) But because there are <u>more on one side</u> than the other there's a steady <u>net flow</u> into the region with <u>fewer</u> water molecules, ie. into the <u>stronger solution</u> (of glucose).
5) This causes the <u>glucose-rich</u> region to <u>fill up with water</u>. The water acts like it's trying to <u>dilute</u> it, so as to "<u>even up</u>" the concentration either side of the membrane.
6) <u>OSMOSIS</u> makes <u>plant</u> cells <u>swell up</u> if they're surrounded by <u>weak solution</u> and they become <u>TURGID</u>. This is real useful for giving <u>support</u> to green plant tissue and for <u>opening stomatal guard cells</u>.
7) <u>Animal</u> cells <u>don't have a cell wall</u> and can easily <u>burst</u> if put into pure water because they <u>take in</u> so much water <u>by osmosis</u>.

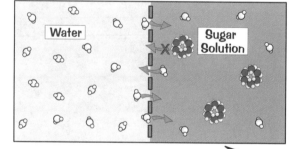

Net movement of water molecules

Turgid plant cell

Animal cell bursting

Learn the facts about Osmosis...

Osmosis can be kind of confusing if you don't get to the bottom of it. In normal diffusion, glucose molecules move, but with small enough holes they can't. That's when only water moves through the membrane, and then it's called <u>osmosis</u>. Easy peasy, I'd say. <u>Learn and enjoy</u>.

Leaf Structure

Leaves are Designed for One Thing Only...
— Making Food by Photosynthesis

The whole structure of leaves is geared towards that. Make sure you learn this diagram with all its labels:

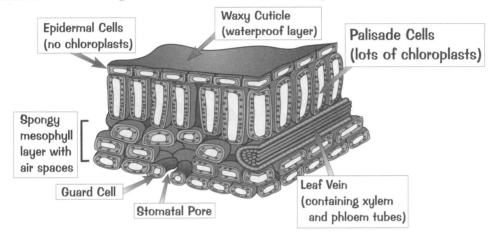

Epidermal Cells (no chloroplasts)

Waxy Cuticle (waterproof layer)

Palisade Cells (lots of chloroplasts)

Spongy mesophyll layer with air spaces

Guard Cell

Stomatal Pore

Leaf Vein (containing xylem and phloem tubes)

Learn all these Important Features about Leaves

1) Leaves are thin and flat to provide a big external surface area to catch lots of sunlight.

2) Epidermal cells are transparent allowing light through to the cells in the palisade layer which are packed with chloroplasts containing lots of chlorophyll. This is where the photosynthesis goes on.

3) Xylem and phloem vessels cover the whole leaf like tiny 'veins', to deliver water and then to take away the food (starch) produced by the leaf.

4) The palisade and spongy layers are full of air spaces to allow CO_2 to reach the palisade cells.

5) The spongy layer has loads of surface area, so gases can quickly diffuse through the leaf and into the cells. In the exam say, "The internal surface area to volume ratio is very large". Nice.

6) The lower surface is full of biddy little holes called stomata. They control how much CO_2 is let into the air spaces. They also allow water to escape — this is how transpiration comes about.

7) There aren't any holes on the upper surface, as too much water would be lost through them. The cells in the epidermis make wax which covers the leaf surface, especially the top surface. This is to limit water loss.

Stomata are Pores which Open and Close Automatically

1) The guard cells control the amount of water in the leaf, by opening and closing the stomatal pores.

2) When there's lots of water at the roots, the guard cells become turgid and change shape, which opens the stomatal pores.

3) The guard cells are the only cells on the bottom of the leaf which contain chloroplasts. In bright light glucose is produced by photosynthesis and water flows into the guard cells by osmosis. The cells become turgid and again the stomatal pores open.

4) When water is scarce or it's dark, the cells become flaccid and they change shape, which closes the stomatal pores.

5) When the pores close, no more water can be lost but no CO_2 can get in either, so photosynthesis in the leaf stops as well.

Cells TURGID, pore OPENS

Cells FLACCID, pore CLOSES

Spend some time poring over these facts...

Two spiffing diagrams and a few simple features. What could be easier? Check the clock and give yourself five minutes of intense active learning to see how much you can learn.

The Transpiration Stream

Transpiration is the loss of water from the Plant

1) It's caused by the evaporation of water from inside the leaves.
2) This creates a slight shortage of water in the leaf which draws more water up from the rest of the plant which in turn draws more up from the roots.
3) It has four beneficial effects:
   a) it transports minerals from the soil.
   b) it cools the plant.
   c) it supplies water for photosynthesis.
   d) it supplies water to maintain turgor pressure and support the plant.

water evaporates
from the leaves

water soaks into the roots

4 Factors which affect it

The rate of transpiration is affected by four things:
1) Amount of light
2) Temperature
3) Amount of air movement
4) Humidity of the surrounding air.

It's surely obvious that the biggest rate of transpiration occurs in hot, dry, windy conditions, ie. perfect clothes-drying weather.

By contrast, a cool, cloudy, muggy day with no wind will produce minimum transpiration.

This constant stream of water has the advantage of transporting vital minerals from the SOIL into the roots and then all around the plant. Plants need to keep taking water from the soil to balance their water loss to stay healthy.

The uptake of water and minerals happens almost entirely at the ROOT HAIRS.

Leaves are good at Photosynthesis, bad at keeping water

1) Plants have evolved to be good at photosynthesis, but the bits of the leaf which make it good at photosynthesis make it bad at keeping water — most water loss happens through the leaves.
2) The stomata which let gas enter the leaf also let water diffuse away.
3) On top of this, the broad flat surface means that lots of sunlight hits the leaf, so more water evaporates.

Turgor Pressure Supports Plant Tissues

1) When a plant is well watered, all its cells will draw water into themselves by osmosis and become turgid.
2) The contents of the cell start to push against the cell wall, like a balloon in a shoebox. Since the cell wall is inelastic (ie. it won't bend or stretch), this water pressure is able to support the plant.
3) Leaves are entirely supported by this turgor pressure. We know this because if there's no water in the soil, a plant starts to wilt and the leaves droop. This is because the cells start to lose water and thus lose their turgor pressure.

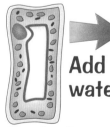

Add water

Flaccid Cell   Turgid Cell

It helps if you're quick on the uptake...

There's quite a lot of information on this page. You could try learning the numbered points, but you'll find a better plan is to do a "mini-essay" on transpiration and write down everything you can think of. Then look back to see what you've forgotten. Then do it again! Till you get it all.

Transport Systems in Plants

Dicotyledonous (ie. bog standard) plants need to transport various things around inside themselves. They have tubes to do this...

Phloem and Xylem Vessels Transport Different Things

1) Plants have two separate sets of tubes for transporting stuff around the plant.
2) Both sets of tubes go to every part of the plant, but they are totally separate.
3) They usually run alongside each other.

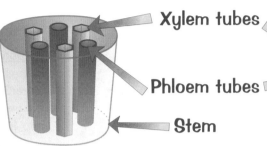

Xylem tubes

Phloem tubes

Stem

Water and food

Phloem Tubes transport Food:

1) Made of living cells with perforated end-plates to allow stuff to flow through.
2) They transport (translocate) food made in the leaves to all other parts of the plant, in both directions.
3) They carry sugars, fats, proteins etc. to growing regions in shoot tips and root tips and to/from storage organs in the roots.

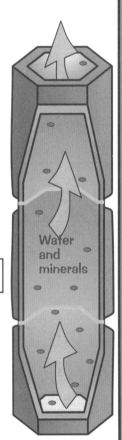

Water and minerals

Xylem Tubes take water UP:

1) Made of dead cells joined end to end with no end walls between them.
2) The side walls are strong and stiff and contain lignin. This gives the plant support.
3) They carry water and minerals from the roots up to the leaves in the transpiration stream.

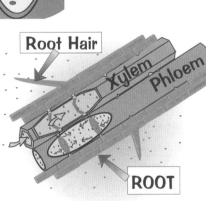

Root Hair

Xylem

Phloem

ROOT

The Phloem and Xylem extend into the Roots

1) The phloem carries starch down to the roots for growth or for storage and may later carry it back up again.
2) The xylem carries water and minerals, (which are taken in by the roots), up to the leaves.

Well that seems to be about the top and bottom of it...

This is an easy page. There are important differences between xylem and phloem tubes. Make sure you know all the numbered points on this page, and the diagrams. Then cover the page and scribble it all down with detailed sketches of the diagrams. Then do it again, and again, until you've learnt it.

Photosynthesis

Photosynthesis Produces Glucose by using Sunlight

1) Photosynthesis is the process that produces 'food' in plants. The 'food' it produces is glucose.
2) Photosynthesis takes place in the leaves of all green plants — this is what leaves are for.

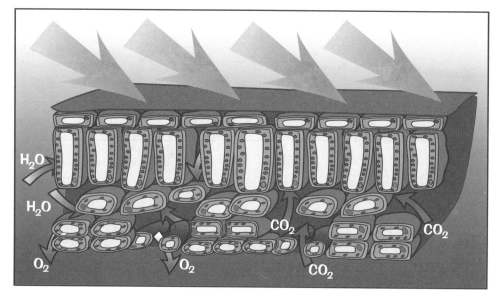

HOW IT ALL WORKS

1) You must have water for photosynthesis — it's supplied to the cells by the leaf veins.

2) Carbon dioxide (CO_2) is the second ingredient — it reaches the cells by diffusing into the leaf.

3) Sunlight provides the energy for the process. The epidermis (top layer of cells) is transparent to let the light enter the leaf.

Learn the Equation for Photosynthesis:

$$\text{Carbon dioxide} + \text{Water} \xrightarrow[\text{chlorophyll}]{\text{SUNLIGHT}} \text{glucose} + \text{oxygen}$$

$$6CO_2 + 6H_2O \xrightarrow[\text{chlorophyll}]{\text{SUNLIGHT}} C_6H_{12}O_6 + 6O_2$$

Higher

Four Things are Needed for Photosynthesis to Happen:

1) Light
Usually from the SUN.

2) Chlorophyll
The green substance which is found in chloroplasts and which makes leaves look green.

This is the 'magic' stuff that makes it all happen. Chlorophyll absorbs the energy in sunlight and uses it to combine CO_2 and WATER to produce GLUCOSE. Oxygen is simply a by-product.

3) Carbon dioxide
Enters the leaf from the AIR around.

4) Water
Comes FROM THE SOIL, up the stem and into the leaf.

Live and Learn...

What you've got to do now is learn everything on this page. Photosynthesis is a "dead cert" for the Exams. On this page you've got two diagrams, two points about photosynthesis and the equations, and then the four necessary conditions. Just keep learning them until you can cover the page and write them all down from memory. Only then will you really know it all.

Altering the Rate of Photosynthesis

The RATE of photosynthesis is affected by THREE FACTORS:

1) THE AMOUNT OF LIGHT (and the wavelength)

The chlorophyll uses light energy to perform photosynthesis. It can only do it as fast as the light energy is arriving. Chlorophyll actually only absorbs the red and blue ends of the visible light spectrum, but not the green light in the middle, which is reflected back. This is why the plant looks green.

2) THE AMOUNT OF CARBON DIOXIDE

CO_2 and water are the raw materials. Water is never really in short supply in a plant but only 0.03% of the air around is CO_2 so it's actually pretty scarce as far as plants are concerned.

3) THE TEMPERATURE

Chlorophyll is like an ENZYME in that it works best when it's warm but not too hot. The rate of photosynthesis depends on how 'happy' the chlorophyll is: WARM but not too hot.

Three Important Graphs For Rate of Photosynthesis

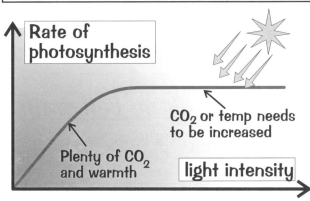

At any given time one or other of the above three factors will be the limiting factor which is keeping the photosynthesis down at the rate it is.

1) If the light level is raised, the rate of photosynthesis will increase steadily but only up to a certain point.

2) Beyond that, it won't make any difference because then it'll be either the temperature or the CO_2 level which is wrong and which is now the limiting factor.

3) Conversely, if the light level is too low, then changing the amount of CO_2 won't increase the rate of photosynthesis at all — not until the light level is raised to match the CO_2 level.

4) To get optimum rate of photosynthesis you need to make sure that
    1) There's enough CO_2
    2) There's plenty of light
    3) The temperature is just right

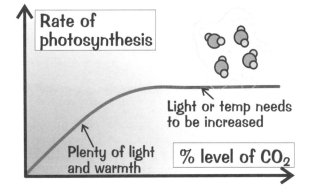

5) Note that you can't really have too much light or CO_2. The temperature however must not get too high or it destroys the chlorophyll enzymes.

6) This happens at about 45°C (which is pretty hot for outdoors, though greenhouses can get that hot if you're not careful).

7) Usually, though, if the temperature is the limiting factor it's because it's too low, and things need warming up a bit.

8) This is why plants grow fastest in the Summer — they've got loads of light and a warm temperature.

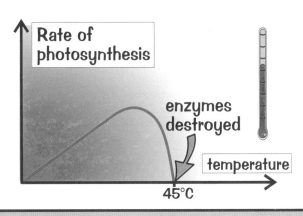

Revision — life isn't all fun and sunshine...

On this page there are three limiting factors, a graph for each and an explanation of why the graphs level off or stop abruptly. Cover the page and practise recalling all these details, until you can do it.

How Plants Use The Glucose

1) Plants <u>manufacture glucose</u> in their <u>leaves</u>.
2) They then use some of the glucose initially for <u>respiration</u>.
3) This <u>releases energy</u> which enables them to <u>convert</u> the rest of the glucose into various <u>other useful substances</u> which they can use to <u>build new cells</u> and <u>grow</u>.
4) To produce some of these substances they also need to <u>gather</u> a few <u>minerals</u> from the soil.

For Respiration ①

Making Fruits ②

<u>GLUCOSE</u> is turned into <u>SUCROSE</u> for storing in <u>FRUITS</u>. Fruits deliberately <u>taste nice</u> so that animals will eat them and so <u>spread the seeds</u> all over the place.

③ Stored in Seeds

<u>GLUCOSE</u> is turned into <u>LIPIDS</u> (fats and oils) for storing in <u>SEEDS</u>. <u>Sunflower seeds</u>, for example, contain a lot of oil — we get <u>cooking oil</u> and <u>margarine</u> from them.

④ For Transport

The <u>ENERGY</u> from <u>GLUCOSE</u> is also needed to <u>transport substances</u> around the plant and for <u>ACTIVE TRANSPORT</u> of <u>minerals</u> in the roots.

⑤ Making Cell walls

<u>GLUCOSE</u> is converted into <u>CELLULOSE</u> for making <u>cell walls</u>, especially in a rapidly growing plant.

⑦ Making Proteins

<u>GLUCOSE</u> is combined with <u>NITRATES</u> (collected from the <u>soil</u>) to make <u>AMINO ACIDS</u>, which are then made into <u>PROTEINS</u>.

⑥ Stored as Starch

<u>Glucose</u> is transported as soluble sugars, then turned into <u>starch</u> and <u>stored</u> in roots, stems and leaves, ready for use when photosynthesis isn't happening, like in the <u>winter</u>.

<u>STARCH</u> is <u>INSOLUBLE</u> which makes it much <u>better</u> for <u>storing</u>, because it doesn't bloat the storage cells by <u>osmosis</u> like glucose would.

<u>Potato and carrot plants</u> store a lot of starch in their roots over the winter to enable a new plant to grow from it the following spring. We eat the swollen roots!

"Sugar it", that's what I say...

There are seven things that plants do with glucose. Can you spot them? If so, <u>learn them</u>, <u>cover the page</u>, and then display your new-found knowledge. In other words, sketch out the diagram and <u>scribble down</u> the seven ways that plants use glucose, including all the extra details.

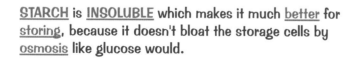

Minerals and Fertilisers

Root Hairs take in Minerals using Active Transport

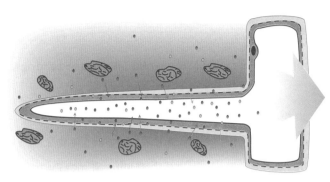

Root Hair cell

1) The cells on plant roots grow into long "hairs" which stick out into the soil.
2) This gives the plant a big surface area for absorbing water, minerals and fertilisers from the soil.
3) The concentration of minerals is higher in the root hair cell than in the soil around it.

4) So, normal diffusion doesn't explain how minerals are taken up into the root hair cell.
5) They should go the other way if they followed the rules of diffusion.
6) The answer is that a conveniently mysterious process called "active transport" is responsible.
7) Active transport allows the plant to absorb minerals against the concentration gradient. This is essential for its growth. But active transport needs energy from respiration to make it work.
8) Active transport also happens in humans, in taking glucose from the gut and kidney tubules.

The Three Essential Minerals

For healthy growth plants need these three really important minerals which they can only obtain from the soil through their roots.

1) Nitrates

— for making AMINO ACIDS and for the "synthesis" (making) of DNA and PROTEINS for cell growth.

2) Phosphates

— have an important role in reactions involved in PHOTOSYNTHESIS and RESPIRATION. The element PHOSPHORUS is also used to make DNA and CELL MEMBRANES.

3) Potassium

— helps the ENZYMES involved in PHOTOSYNTHESIS and RESPIRATION to work.

Fertilisers contain all three of these minerals, plus iron and magnesium...

Iron and Magnesium are also needed in Small Amounts

The three main minerals are needed in fairly large amounts, but there are other elements which are needed in much smaller amounts. IRON and MAGNESIUM are the most significant as they're required for making CHLOROPHYLL, which is pretty important to plants, in case you didn't know.

Just relax and soak up the information...

Very straightforward learning here. Two nice big clear sections with all the important bits highlighted in colour as usual. You should be able to cover this page and scribble virtually the whole thing down again with very little bother. Learn and enjoy.

Revision Summary For Module BD5

There's a lot of real easy stuff on plants, that's for sure. But easy stuff means easy marks, and you better make sure you get all the easy marks — every last one. There's nothing quite as spectacularly dumb as working really hard at the difficult stuff and then forgetting about the easy bits. Here are some tough questions on plants for you. Practise them over and over and over until you can just glide through them all, like a swan or something.

1) Sketch a typical plant and label the five important parts. Explain exactly what each bit does.

2) Which two parts of the plant hold it upright?

3) Give the strict definition of diffusion. Sketch how a smell diffuses through air in a room.

4) Which three gases diffuse in and out of leaves? What process are they involved with?

5) Why are cell membranes kinda clever? What will and won't diffuse through cell membranes?

6) Give the full strict definition of osmosis. What does it do to plant and animal cells in water?

7) What is Visking tubing? What will and won't pass through it?

8) Sketch the cross-section of a leaf with seven labels. What is the leaf for?

9) Why are leaves thin and flat?

10) Why are the epidermal cells of the leaf transparent?

11) Which part of the leaf has a large internal surface area to volume ratio? Why is this ratio so large?

12) How does water get into the leaf?

13) Explain what stomata do and how they do it.

14) What is transpiration? What causes it?

15) What benefits does transpiration bring to the plant?

16) What are the four factors which affect the rate of transpiration?

17) Most water loss occurs through the leaves. Give two reasons for this.

18) What is turgor pressure? How does it come about and what use is it to plants?

19) What are the two types of tubes in plants? Whereabouts are they found in plants?

20) List three features of both types of tube and sketch them both.

21) What does photosynthesis do? Where does it do it?

22) Write down the word and symbol equations for photosynthesis.

23) Sketch a leaf and show the four things needed for photosynthesis.

24) What are the three variable quantities which affect the rate of photosynthesis?

25) Sketch a graph for each one and explain the shape.

26) Describe conditions where each of the three factors is in short supply.

27) Sketch a plant and label the seven ways that plants use glucose.

28) Give a couple of extra details for each of the seven uses.

29) What happens at the root hairs? What process is involved? Which process won't work there?

30) List the three essential minerals needed for healthy plant growth, and say what they're needed for.

31) Where do plants get these essential minerals from?

32) What two minerals are needed for making chlorophyll?

Respiration

It may come as a shock, but respiration <u>doesn't</u> mean breathing in and out — there's a bit more to it than that. I know what you're thinking — there's always more to it than that. But anyway... that's life, I reckon.

Respiration is NOT "breathing in and out"

1) Respiration is <u>NOT</u> breathing in and breathing out, as you might think.

2) <u>Respiration</u> actually goes on in <u>every cell</u> in your body.

3) <u>Respiration</u> is the process of converting <u>glucose</u> to <u>energy</u>.

4) This energy is used to: build up <u>larger molecules</u> (like proteins)

                             contract <u>muscles</u>

                             maintain a steady <u>body temperature</u>

5) <u>Plants</u> respire too. All living things "<u>respire</u>". They convert <u>food from light</u> into <u>energy</u>.

> ### RESPIRATION is the process of CONVERTING GLUCOSE TO ENERGY, which goes on IN EVERY CELL

Aerobic Respiration Needs Plenty of Oxygen

1) <u>Aerobic respiration</u> is what happens if there's <u>plenty of oxygen</u> available.

2) "<u>Aerobic</u>" just means "<u>with oxygen</u>" and it's the ideal way to convert <u>glucose</u> into <u>energy</u>.

You need to learn <u>the word equation</u>:

$$\text{Glucose} + \text{Oxygen} \rightarrow \text{Carbon Dioxide} + \text{Water} + \text{Energy}$$

..and <u>the chemical equation</u>:

$$C_6H_{12}O_6 + 6O_2 \rightarrow 6CO_2 + 6H_2O + \text{Energy}$$

Anaerobic Respiration doesn't use Oxygen at all

1) <u>Anaerobic respiration</u> is what happens if there's <u>no oxygen available</u>.

2) "<u>An</u>aerobic" just means "<u>without</u> oxygen". It's the <u>incomplete</u> breakdown of glucose which is <u>NOT</u> <u>the best way to convert glucose into energy</u> because it produces lactic acid.

You need to learn <u>the word equation</u>:

$$\text{Glucose} \rightarrow \text{Energy} + \text{Lactic Acid}$$

3) <u>Anaerobic respiration</u> does <u>not produce nearly as much energy</u> as aerobic respiration — but it's useful in emergencies.

One Big Deep Breath and LEARN IT...

There are three sections on this page and learning them well enough to <u>scribble them down</u> from <u>memory</u> isn't so difficult. Try to visualise the basic page layout and remember how many numbered points there are for each bit. You don't have to write it out word for word, just make sure you remember the important points.

More About Respiration

When you run about a lot, you start to breathe more heavily — and you'd probably like to know why this is. If so, learn the stuff on this page. If not, learn it anyway, since you need to know it for the Exam.

Exercise and the Oxygen Debt

1) When you do vigorous exercise and your body can't supply enough <u>oxygen</u> to your muscles they start doing <u>anaerobic respiration</u> instead.

2) This isn't great because <u>lactic acid</u> builds up in the muscles, which gets <u>painful</u>.

3) The advantage is that at least you can keep on using your muscles for a while longer.

4) After resorting to anaerobic respiration, when you stop you'll have an <u>oxygen debt</u>.

5) In other words you have to "<u>repay</u>" the oxygen that you didn't get to your muscles in time, because your <u>lungs</u>, <u>heart</u> and <u>blood</u> couldn't keep up with the <u>demand</u> earlier on.

6) This means you have to keep breathing hard for a while <u>after you stop</u> to get oxygen into your muscles to oxidise the painful lactic acid to harmless CO_2 and water.

Carbon Dioxide Must be Removed from the Body

1) <u>Carbon dioxide</u> is the waste product of aerobic respiration and <u>must be removed</u>.

2) It is <u>toxic</u> in high enough quantities, so it is <u>removed</u> by the <u>lungs</u> through breathing.

3) When <u>high levels</u> of CO_2 and <u>lactic acid</u> are detected in the blood (by the brain), the <u>pulse</u> and <u>breathing rate</u> are <u>both increased automatically</u> to try and rectify the situation.

4) A good measure of fitness is how quickly you can <u>recover</u> to normal breathing and pulse after doing some vigorous exercise. This is called your <u>recovery time</u>.

Composition of Inhaled and Exhaled Air

The air you <u>breathe in</u> and the air you <u>breathe out</u> are not the same — <u>inhaled</u> air and <u>exhaled</u> air have different amounts of <u>carbon dioxide</u> and <u>oxygen</u>.

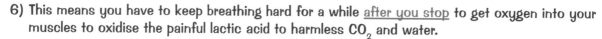

INHALED AIR	EXHALED AIR
1) 79% Nitrogen.	1) 79% Nitrogen.
2) 21% Oxygen.	2) 17% Oxygen.
3) 0.03% Carbon Dioxide.	3) 4% Carbon Dioxide.
4) Cooler than exhaled air.	4) Contains more moisture than inhaled air.

1) About <u>79%</u> of air is <u>nitrogen</u>. This percentage is the <u>same</u> for both <u>inhaled</u> and <u>exhaled</u> air, as your body doesn't use nitrogen from the air.

2) The amount of <u>oxygen used</u> matches the amount of <u>CO_2 produced</u> (as in the aerobic respiration equation on page 29).

3) Notice that even with millions of alveoli, you still only absorb a <u>small proportion</u> of the <u>oxygen</u> in each breath.

Let's see what you know then...

Read the page then see what you can <u>scribble down</u> about each of the three sections. <u>Then try again</u>. You don't want to try and learn those six points about "Oxygen Debt" too formally. It's much better to write your own mini-essay on it and then see what stuff you missed. Enjoy.

Homeostasis

Homeostasis is a fancy word. It covers a lot of things, so I guess it has to be. Homeostasis covers all the functions of your body which try to maintain a "constant internal environment". Learn the definition:

HOMEOSTASIS – the maintenance of a CONSTANT INTERNAL ENVIRONMENT

There are <u>six different bodily levels</u> that need to be controlled by <u>balancing</u> body <u>inputs</u> and <u>outputs</u>:

1) REMOVAL OF CO_2
2) REMOVAL OF <u>UREA</u> } ← These two are <u>wastes</u>. They're constantly produced in the body and <u>you just need to get rid of them</u>.
3) <u>Water</u> content
4) <u>Sugar</u> content
5) <u>Temperature</u>
6) <u>Oxygen</u> } ← These four are all <u>"goodies"</u> and we need them, <u>but at just the right level</u> — not too much and not too little.

Negative Feedback Keeps Things In Check

Negative feedback is when something happens that <u>triggers another action</u> which <u>inhibits the original thing</u>. A good example is a room <u>thermostat</u>. Once the room is heated to the right temperature, the thermostat <u>reduces</u> the heating. When the room <u>cools</u>, it turns it up again. This is negative feedback in action, and our <u>bodies</u> have various similar negative feedback mechanisms looking after our <u>homeostasis</u>.

Higher

Learn the Organs Involved in Homeostasis:

Pituitary Gland
Produces many vital hormones, including <u>ADH</u>, for controlling <u>water content</u>.

The Brain
1) Contains receptors to monitor <u>blood temperature</u> and <u>water content</u> and then sends <u>nerve impulses</u> to the <u>skin</u> and to the <u>pituitary gland</u>.
2) It also <u>monitors CO_2</u> levels.

The Skin
This <u>removes water</u> through <u>sweat</u> and adjusts the <u>body temperature</u>, with the help of...

The Muscles
which can produce <u>heat</u> if necessary (by <u>shivering</u>).

The Lungs
These <u>remove CO_2</u> and some of the <u>excess water</u>.

The Kidneys
<u>Remove urea</u>. They also adjust the <u>ion</u> and <u>water content</u> of the blood.

The Liver
The Pancreas
These two <u>work together</u> to adjust <u>blood sugar level</u>.

The Bladder
This is where <u>urine</u> is stored before departure.

Learn about Homeostasis — and keep your cool...
This is all a bit technical. Homeostasis is really quite a complicated business. It's just a good job it does it automatically or we'd all be in real trouble. You still gotta <u>learn it</u> for your Exam though.

Skin and Temperature

Controlling Our Body Temperature

All enzymes work best at a certain temperature. The enzymes within the human body work best at about 37°C. The heat released by respiration is used to keep body temperature at 37°C.

When you're too cold you shiver. The muscles contract repeatedly to produce heat by respiration.

When you're too hot you produce sweat. The evaporation of sweat requires heat, so it takes heat away from the body, cooling you down.

You then need to get the lost water back by drinking.

1) There is a thermoregulatory centre in the brain which acts as your own personal thermostat.

2) It contains receptors that are sensitive to the blood temperature in the brain.

3) The thermoregulatory (there's that long word again) centre also receives impulses from the skin.

4) These impulses provide information about skin temperature.

The Skin has Three Tricks for Altering Body Temperature

1) The skin is very important for keeping the human body at 37°C.
2) The thermoregulatory centre senses changes and sends nervous impulses to the skin.
3) Sweating, blood supply and what the hairs are doing help control body temperature:

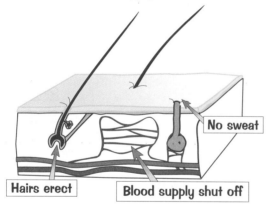

No sweat

Hairs erect   Blood supply shut off

When you're TOO COLD:

1) Hairs stand on end to keep you warm by trapping air underneath.
2) No sweat is produced.
3) The blood supply to the skin closes off so less heat is released through the skin.
   This is vasoconstriction — it means the capillaries under the surface of the skin get narrower so less blood can pass through them.

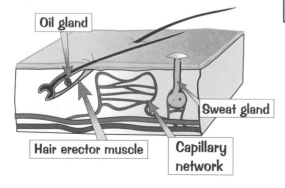

Oil gland

Sweat gland

Hair erector muscle   Capillary network

When you're TOO HOT:

1) Hairs lie flat.
2) Sweat is produced which evaporates to cool you down. Heat is lost since the sweat requires heat from the skin to evaporate.
3) The blood supply to the skin opens up to release body heat through the skin.
   This is vasodilation — it means the capillaries get wider so more blood can pass through them.

So much to learn — don't let it get under your skin...

There are lots of important facts to learn on this page, plus a couple of suitably splendid diagrams. Learn the headings for each section, then cover the page and scribble out the details. Have a go at the diagrams as well, they're important and won't take long just to sketch.

Kidneys

Kidneys are essential for removing <u>wastes</u>, and <u>excess salt</u> and <u>water</u> from the blood.

Kidneys basically act as Filters to "Clean the Blood"

The <u>kidneys</u> perform <u>three main roles</u>:

1) *<u>Removal of urea</u>* from the blood.
2) *<u>Adjustment of salt</u>* in the blood.
3) *<u>Adjustment of water content</u>* of the blood.

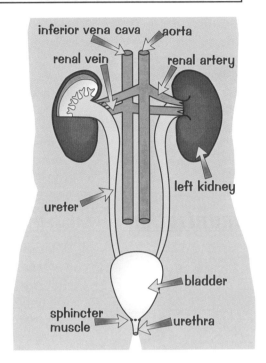

1) Removal of Urea

1) <u>Urea</u> is produced in the <u>liver</u>.

2) Proteins can't be <u>stored</u> by the body so <u>excess amino acids</u> are <u>broken down</u> by the liver into fats and carbohydrates.

3) The <u>waste product</u> is urea, which is passed into the blood to be <u>filtered out</u> by the <u>kidneys</u>. Urea is also lost partly in <u>sweat</u>. Urea is <u>poisonous</u>, so it needs to be removed from the body.

2) Adjustment of Salt Content

1) <u>Ions</u> such as sodium are taken into the body in <u>food</u>, and then absorbed into the blood.

2) Excess ions are <u>removed</u> by the kidneys. For example, a salty meal will contain far too much salt and the kidneys will <u>remove the excess salt ions</u> from the blood.

3) Some ions are also lost in <u>sweat</u> (which tastes salty, you'll have noticed).

4) But the important thing to remember is that the <u>balance</u> is always maintained by the <u>kidneys</u>.

3) Adjustment of Water Content

Water is <u>taken</u> into the body as <u>food and drink</u> and is <u>lost</u> from the body in <u>four ways</u>:
     1) in <u>urine</u>, 2) in <u>sweat</u>, 3) in <u>breath</u>, 4) in <u>faeces</u>.

There's a need for the body to <u>constantly balance</u> the water coming in against the water going out.
The amount lost in the <u>breath</u> is fairly <u>constant</u>, which means the <u>water balance</u> is between:
     1) Liquids <u>consumed</u>,
     2) Amount <u>sweated out</u>,
     3) Amount <u>dumped by the kidneys</u> into the <u>urine</u>.

<u>On a cold day</u>, if you <u>don't sweat</u>, you'll produce <u>more urine</u> which will be <u>pale and dilute</u>.
<u>On a hot day</u>, you <u>sweat a lot</u>, and so your urine will be <u>dark-coloured</u>, <u>concentrated</u> and <u>little of it</u>.
The water lost through sweat has to be taken in as food and drink to <u>restore the balance</u>.

A joke about kidneys? — Better keep it clean...

Do the usual thing — sit and <u>learn it</u>, then <u>cover the page</u> and <u>sketch out the diagrams</u> and <u>scribble down</u> all the important details. Then try again, and again, until you get it all.
I hope it's obvious that you only scribble out very rough diagrams — just to show the details.

Fighting Disease

Once micro-organisms have entered our bodies they will reproduce rapidly unless they are destroyed. Your 'immune system' does just that, and white blood cells are the most important part of it.

Your Immune System: White blood cells

They travel around in your blood and crawl into every part of you, constantly patrolling for micro-organisms. When they come across an invading micro-organism they have two lines of attack:

1) Consuming Them

White blood cells can engulf foreign cells and digest them.

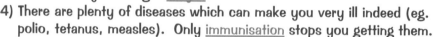

Microbes / White Blood Cell

2) Producing Antibodies

When your white blood cells come across an antigen (foreign cell) they will start to produce proteins called antibodies to kill the new invading cells. The antibodies are then produced rapidly and flow all round the body to lock on to all similar bacteria or viruses and kill them. Each disease organism has its own antigens and needs specific antibodies to kill it.

Immunisation — Getting antibodies ready for attack

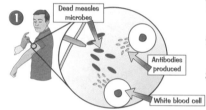

1) Once your white cells have produced antibodies to tackle a new strain of bacteria or viruses you have what's called "natural immunity" to it.
2) This means if the same micro-organisms attack again they'll be killed by the antibodies you already have for them, and you won't get ill.
3) The trouble is when a new micro-organism appears, it takes your white blood cells a few days to produce the antibodies to deal with them and in that time you can get very ill.
4) There are plenty of diseases which can make you very ill indeed (eg. polio, tetanus, measles). Only immunisation stops you getting them.
5) Immunisation involves injecting dead micro-organisms into you. This causes your body to produce antibodies to attack them, even though they're dead. They can do no harm to you because they're dead.
6) If live micro-organisms of the same type appeared after that, they'd be killed immediately by the antibodies which you have already developed against them. Cool.

Three Ways our Bodies Defend Against Disease-Organisms

1) The Skin and Eyes

Undamaged skin is a very effective barrier against micro-organisms. If it gets damaged, the blood clots quickly to seal cuts and keep micro-organisms out. Eyes produce a chemical which kills bacteria on the surface of the eye.

A horrid Flu Virus

2) The Digestive System

Contaminated food and dirty water allow micro-organisms to enter your body. The stomach produces strong hydrochloric acid which kills most micro-organisms which enter that way.

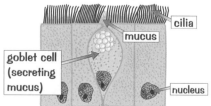

cilia / mucus / goblet cell (secreting mucus) / nucleus

3) The Breathing System

The whole respiratory tract (nasal passage, trachea and lungs) is lined with a mucous membrane and cilia (tiny little hairs) which catch dust and bacteria before they reach the lungs.

Fighting disease the Bruce Lee way...

If Bruce Lee were a body part he would definitely be a white blood cell. They're lean, mean fighting machines. Mini-essay for this section I think. Make sure you learn all the numbered points first.

Drugs

1) Drugs are substances which alter the way the body works. Some drugs are useful of course, for example antibiotics such as penicillin. However there are many drugs which are <u>dangerous</u> if misused, and many of them are <u>addictive</u> or "habit-forming".

2) The loss of control and judgement caused by many drugs can easily lead to <u>death</u> from various other causes, eg. getting HIV or hepatitis from used needles, choking on vomit, wrapping the car around a tree at 60 mph, etc.... Horrible, horrible things.

Addiction and Withdrawal Symptoms

1) There's a difference between true <u>chemical addiction</u> and <u>psychological addiction</u>.

2) In <u>chemical addiction</u> the body becomes adjusted to the constant presence of the drug in the system. If the drug is withdrawn, there are various <u>unpleasant physical withdrawal symptoms</u>: fevers, hallucinations, nausea, and the shakes.

3) If the user keeps taking the drug then their <u>tolerance</u> to the drug <u>increases</u>, so they need a <u>larger dose</u> to get the same effect, which is <u>very dangerous</u>.

4) <u>Psychological addiction</u> is habit — where the person "feels the need" to keep taking the drug.

Stimulants Speed up Brain Activity

1) <u>Stimulants</u> tend to make the nervous system generally more alert and "awake".

2) <u>Caffeine</u> is a <u>mild stimulant</u> found in tea and coffee. It's pretty harmless. Few lives are wrecked by obsessive tea-drinking. <u>Nicotine</u> is also a <u>stimulant</u> — it's definitely more dangerous than tea though. See the section about tobacco and smoking on the next page.

3) However, amphetamine and methedrine are also stimulants. Strong stimulants like these produce a feeling of boundless energy, but users experience <u>serious depression</u> if they stop taking them. An unhealthy <u>dependence</u> develops all too easily. Continued use can lead to severe paranoid delusions.

Stimulants act in two ways.
1) They <u>cause more neurotransmitter</u> to be released at the <u>synapses</u>. (<u>Neurotransmitter</u> is the chemical which transfers nervous impulses across your synapses — see module BD2.)
2) They make the brain remove less neurotransmitter. Either way, they cause more neurotransmitter to wash around in the brain. This speeds up <u>brain activity</u>, and <u>increases</u> feelings of <u>alertness</u> or <u>pleasure</u>.

Depressants Slow You Down

<u>Depressants</u> tend to slow down the responses of the nervous system, causing <u>slow reactions</u> and poor judgement of speed, distances, etc. <u>Solvents</u> and <u>alcohol</u> are both depressants.

Depressants act by <u>inhibiting neurotransmitter</u> release at the <u>synapses</u>. This <u>slows down</u> reactions and makes the person taking them less responsive. They can also affect parts of the brain which control mood. <u>Alcohol</u>, for example can cause <u>mood changes</u> and <u>lessen inhibitions</u>.

Solvents are Depressants

1) <u>Solvents</u> are found in a variety of "household" items eg. glues, paints.
2) They are <u>dangerous</u> and have many <u>damaging effects</u> on both body and personality.
3) They <u>slow down brain</u> activity, like all <u>depressants</u>.
4) They cause <u>hallucinations</u> and adversely affect <u>personality and behaviour</u>.
5) They cause <u>damage</u> to the <u>lungs</u>, <u>brain</u>, <u>liver</u> and <u>kidney</u>.

Learn about these drugs and then forget them...

Anyone with half a brain avoids these drugs like they do <u>rat fleas</u>.
Enjoy your life, instead of being a sucker.

Drugs

1) Alcohol and tobacco are the two main (non-medical) drugs which are legal in this country.
2) But don't be fooled. They can do you a lot of harm just like the other drugs can.

Alcohol Affects Reaction Times, Liver and Brain

1) The main effect of alcohol is to reduce the activity of the nervous system. The positive aspect of this is that it makes us feel less inhibited. Alcohol in moderation helps people to socialise and relax. The great danger however is impaired judgement and very slow reaction times — a combination which leads to drunk driving and the death of innocent people.

2) However, if you let alcohol take over, it can wreck your life. And it does. It wrecks a lot of people's lives. You have to control it.

3) If alcohol starts to take over someone's life there are many harmful effects:

   a) Alcohol is basically poisonous. The liver has to work hard to remove it from the body. Too much drinking will cause severe damage to the liver and the brain.

   b) Too much alcohol impairs judgement, which can cause accidents, and it can also severely affect the person's work and home life.

   c) Serious dependency on alcohol will eventually lead to loss of job, loss of income and the start of a severe downward spiral.

Smoking Tobacco

Smoking is no good to anyone except the cigarette companies.
And once you've started smoking there's no going back. It's a one way trip, pal.

You'll notice that smokers are no happier than non-smokers, even when they're smoking. What may start off as something "different" to do, rapidly becomes something they have to do, just to feel OK. But non-smokers feel just as OK without spending £20 or more each week and wrecking their health into the bargain.

And why do people start smoking? To look the part, that's why. They have an image in their head of how they want to appear and smoking seems the perfect fashion accessory.

Well just remember, it's a one-way trip. You might think it makes you look cool at 16, but will it still seem the perfect fashion accessory when you're 20 with a new group of friends who don't smoke? Nope. Too late. You're stuck with it.

And by the time you're 60 it'll have cost you over £60,000. Enough to buy a Ferrari. That's quite an expensive fashion accessory. Smoking? Cool?
Oh yeah — it's about as cool as cool can be, I'd say.

DEATH TUBES

WARNING
SMOKING CAUSES:
WRINKLED AND THIN SKIN
HAIR LOSS
STAINED TEETH AND FINGERS
BREATHLESSNESS
BAD BREATH
GUM DISEASE
EMPHYSEMA
BRONCHITIS
LUNG CANCER
HEART DISEASE

Oh and by the way...

Tobacco smoke does this inside your body:
1) It coats the inside of your lungs with tar so they become hideously inefficient.
2) Ciliated epithelial cells have little hairs/cilia on them for removing mucus from the lungs. Tobacco smoke coats these in tar preventing them from getting bacteria and mucus out of your lungs. Because the mucus stays in the lungs this leads to a "smoker's cough".
3) It causes disease of the heart and blood vessels, leading to heart attacks and strokes.
4) It causes lung cancer. Out of every ten lung cancer patients, nine of them smoke.

Smoking stains teeth yellow.

5) It causes severe loss of lung function leading to diseases like emphysema and bronchitis, in which the insides of the lungs are basically wrecked. People with severe bronchitis can't manage even a brisk walk, because their lungs can't get enough oxygen into the blood. It kills over 20,000 people in Britain every year.

6) Carbon monoxide in tobacco smoke stops haemoglobin carrying as much oxygen. In pregnant women this deprives the foetus of oxygen, leading to a small baby at birth. In short, "smoking chokes your baby".

7) But this is the best bit. The effect of the nicotine is negligible — other than to make you addicted to it. It doesn't make you high — just dependent. Great.

Learn the Numbered Points for your Exam...

It's the disease aspects they concentrate on most in the Exams. Learn the rest for a nice life.

Revision Summary for Module BD6

Module BD6 has got all sorts of grisly bits and bobs in it. And some of it can be really quite hard to understand too. But it's all worth points in the Exam, and what do points mean? Prizes! These questions are designed to test what you know. They're pretty tough I grant you, but they really are the best way of revising. Keep trying these questions any time you feel like it, and for any you can't do, look back in BD6 and learn the answer to it for next time.

1) What is "respiration"? Give a proper definition.

2) What is "aerobic respiration"? Give the word and symbol equation for it.

3) What is "anaerobic respiration"? Give the word equation for what happens in our bodies.

4) Why can your muscles hurt during vigorous exercise? What is the oxygen debt?

5) What is the proper definition for homeostasis? What are the six bodily levels involved?

6) Draw a diagram of the body showing the eight organs involved in homeostasis.

7) Say exactly what each of these organs does to help.

8) What is a negative feedback system? Give an example of a body level controlled in this way.

9) What temperature do the enzymes in our body prefer?

10) Which organ detects body temperature? How does it tell the skin about it?

11) Draw diagrams showing the three things the skin does when we're a) too hot b) too cold.

12) What are vasoconstriction and vasodilation?
    How does vasodilation remove heat from the body?

13) What is the basic function of the kidneys? What *three* particular things do they deal with?

14) Explain in detail exactly what the kidney does in relation to each of these three things.

15) Draw a labelled diagram to show where the kidneys are located in the body.

16) What happens to your urine on cold days?

17) What about on hot days? Why does this happen?

18) What is meant by your "immune system"? What is the most important part of it?

19) List the two ways that white blood cells deal with invading micro-organisms.

20) Give full details of the process of immunisation. How does it work?

21) Give details of three ways that our body prevents organisms from entering us.

22) What are the two types of addiction?

23) Give an example of a stimulant and an example of a depressant.
    Describe the ways that depressants and stimulants affect brain activity.

24) Explain the dangers of drinking alcohol.

25) Explain why smoking is just *so cool* — *not.*

26) List in detail all six major health problems that result from smoking.

Covalent Bonding

Covalent bonding is when atoms <u>share</u> electrons. This happens really often with <u>non-metals</u>.

Covalent Bonds — Sharing Electrons

1) Sometimes atoms make <u>covalent bonds</u> by <u>sharing</u> electrons with other atoms.
2) This way <u>both</u> atoms feel that they have a <u>full outer shell</u>, and that makes them happy.
3) Each <u>covalent bond</u> provides <u>one extra shared electron</u> for each atom.
4) Each atom involved has to make <u>enough</u> covalent bonds to <u>fill up</u> its outer shell.
5) <u>Learn</u> these <u>seven important examples</u>:

1) Hydrogen, H_2

Hydrogen atoms only <u>need one more electron</u> to complete the first shell...

...so they form a <u>single covalent bond</u> to achieve this, ie. they share <u>one pair</u> of electrons.

2) Chlorine, Cl_2

Chlorine bonds in the <u>same way</u> as <u>hydrogen</u>.

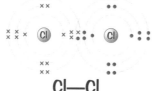

Each chlorine atom shares <u>one</u> of its electrons and they both end up with <u>full outer shells</u>.

3) Methane, CH_4

Carbon has <u>four outer electrons</u>, which is a <u>half full</u> shell.

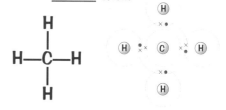

To become a 4+ or a 4– ion is hard work, so it forms <u>four covalent bonds</u> to make up its outer shell.

4) Oxygen Gas, O_2 and 5) Water, H_2O

The <u>oxygen</u> atom has <u>six</u> outer electrons. Sometimes it forms <u>ionic</u> bonds by <u>taking</u> two electrons to complete the outer shell. However it will also cheerfully form <u>covalent bonds</u> and <u>share</u> two electrons instead, as in <u>oxygen gas</u> (O_2) and <u>water molecules</u> (where it <u>shares</u> electrons with the H atoms).

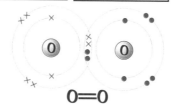

OXYGEN GAS

Two pairs of electrons are shared, so it's a <u>double bond</u>.

WATER

Each bond involves <u>one pair</u> of electrons, so they're <u>single bonds</u>.

6) Carbon Dioxide, CO_2

Carbon has <u>four</u> electrons in its outer shell, and needs <u>four more</u> to fill it up.

Each oxygen atom needs <u>two</u> electrons for a full outer shell. So <u>two double bonds</u> are formed. A double bond means that <u>two pairs</u> of electrons are shared.

7) Ethene, C_2H_4

The <u>carbon</u> atoms form a <u>double bond</u> with each other, and <u>single bonds</u> with <u>two</u> hydrogen atoms each.
This gives <u>all</u> the atoms a <u>full outer shell</u>.

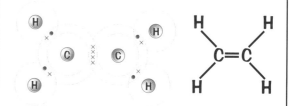

Full Shells — you just can't beat them...

<u>Learn</u> all the points about covalent bonds plus the <u>examples</u>. Then turn over and scribble it down again. Make sure you can <u>draw</u> all six molecules and explain <u>why</u> they bond like they do.

Covalent Substances: Two Kinds

Substances formed from <u>covalent bonds</u> can either be <u>simple molecules</u> or <u>giant structures</u>.

Simple Molecular Substances

1) The covalent bonds <u>between the atoms</u> in these <u>small molecules</u> are <u>very strong</u>.

2) By contrast, the forces of attraction <u>between</u> the molecules are <u>very weak</u>.

3) The <u>result</u> of these <u>feeble inter-molecular forces</u> is that the <u>melting</u> and <u>boiling points</u> are <u>very low</u>, because the molecules are <u>easily parted</u> from each other.

4) Most molecular substances are <u>gases or liquids</u> at room temperature.

5) Molecular substances <u>don't conduct electricity</u>, simply because there are <u>no free ions</u>.

6) They <u>don't dissolve in water</u>, usually.

7) You can usually tell a molecular substance just from its <u>physical state</u>, which is always kinda "<u>mushy</u>" — ie. <u>liquid</u> or <u>gas</u> or an <u>easily-melted solid</u>.

Very weak inter-molecular forces

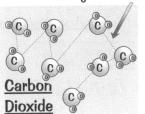

Carbon Dioxide

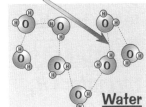

Water

Giant Covalent Structures

1) These are similar to giant ionic structures except that there are <u>no charged ions</u>.

2) <u>All</u> the atoms are <u>bonded</u> to <u>each other</u> by <u>strong</u> covalent bonds.

3) This gives them <u>very high</u> melting and boiling points.

4) They <u>don't conduct electricity</u> — not even when <u>molten</u>.

5) They're usually <u>insoluble</u> in water.

6) The <u>main examples</u> are <u>Graphite</u> and <u>Diamond</u>, which are both made only from <u>carbon atoms</u>. Buckminster Fullerene is also a form of pure carbon.

Graphite

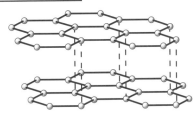

1) Each carbon atom only forms <u>three covalent bonds</u>, creating <u>sheets of carbon atoms</u> which are free to <u>slide over each other</u>.

2) This makes graphite really <u>soft</u> and ideal as a <u>lubricating material</u>.

3) Also as only three out of each carbon's four outer electrons are used in bonds, there are lots of <u>spare electrons</u>. This means that graphite <u>conducts electricity</u> — the <u>only non-metal</u> that does.

Diamond

1) Each carbon atom forms <u>four covalent bonds</u> in a <u>very rigid</u> giant covalent structure, which makes diamond <u>really hard</u>.

2) It <u>doesn't conduct electricity</u> because there are <u>no free electrons</u>.

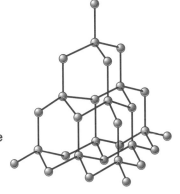

Buckminster Fullerene

1) Sixty <u>carbon atoms</u> joined in a big ball.

2) Each carbon atom forms three covalent bonds.

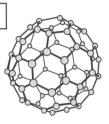

Come on — pull yourself together...

There are two types of covalently bonded substances — and they're totally different. Make sure you know all the details about them and the examples too. <u>This is real basic stuff</u> — just easy marks to be won... or lost. <u>Cover the page</u> and see how many marks you're gonna <u>win</u>.

Alkanes and Alkenes

Hydrocarbons are substances containing just hydrogen and carbon.
Alkanes and alkenes are two types of hydrocarbon. Know the differences between them.

ALKANES have all C–C SINGLE bonds

1) They're made up of chains of carbon atoms with SINGLE COVALENT BONDS.
2) They're called saturated hydrocarbons because they have no spare bonds left.
3) This is also why they don't decolourise bromine water — no spare bonds. ◄ (See next page for more info about this.)
4) They won't form polymers — same reason again, no spare bonds.
5) The first four alkanes are methane (natural gas), ethane, propane and butane.
6) They burn cleanly producing carbon dioxide and water.

1) Methane
Formula: CH_4

$$H-\underset{\underset{H}{|}}{\overset{\overset{H}{|}}{C}}-H$$ (natural gas)

2) Ethane
Formula: C_2H_6

$$H-\underset{\underset{H}{|}}{\overset{\overset{H}{|}}{C}}-\underset{\underset{H}{|}}{\overset{\overset{H}{|}}{C}}-H$$

3) Propane
Formula: C_3H_8

$$H-\underset{\underset{H}{|}}{\overset{\overset{H}{|}}{C}}-\underset{\underset{H}{|}}{\overset{\overset{H}{|}}{C}}-\underset{\underset{H}{|}}{\overset{\overset{H}{|}}{C}}-H$$

4) Butane
Formula: C_4H_{10}

$$H-\underset{\underset{H}{|}}{\overset{\overset{H}{|}}{C}}-\underset{\underset{H}{|}}{\overset{\overset{H}{|}}{C}}-\underset{\underset{H}{|}}{\overset{\overset{H}{|}}{C}}-\underset{\underset{H}{|}}{\overset{\overset{H}{|}}{C}}-H$$

ALKENES have a C=C DOUBLE bond

1) They're chains of carbon atoms with ONE DOUBLE BOND.
2) They are called unsaturated hydrocarbons because they have some spare bonds left.
3) This is why they will decolourise bromine water. They form bonds with bromide ions. ◄ (See next page for more info about this.)
4) They form polymers by opening up their double bonds to 'hold hands' in a long chain.
5) The first three alkenes are ethene, propene and butene.
6) They tend to burn with a smoky flame, producing soot (carbon).

1) Ethene
Formula: C_2H_4

$$\underset{H}{\overset{H}{\diagdown}}C=C\underset{\diagdown H}{\overset{\diagup H}{}}$$

2) Propene
Formula: C_3H_6

$$H-\underset{\underset{H}{|}}{\overset{\overset{H}{|}}{C}}-\underset{\underset{H}{|}}{\overset{\overset{H}{|}}{C}}=C\underset{\diagdown H}{\overset{\diagup H}{}}$$

3) Butene
Formula: C_4H_8

$$H-\underset{\underset{H}{|}}{\overset{\overset{H}{|}}{C}}-\underset{\underset{H}{|}}{\overset{\overset{H}{|}}{C}}=C-\underset{\underset{H}{|}}{\overset{\overset{H}{|}}{C}}-H$$

Important Notes to be noted:

1) Bromine water is the standard test to distinguish between alkanes and alkenes. (See next page.)
2) Alkenes are more reactive due to the double bond all poised and ready to just pop open.
3) Notice the names: "Meth-" means "one carbon atom"; "eth-" means "two C atoms"; "prop-" means "three C atoms"; "but-" means "four C atoms", etc. The only difference then between the names of alkanes and alkenes is just the "-ane" or "-ene" on the end.
4) All alkanes have the formula: C_nH_{2n+2} All alkenes have the formula: C_nH_{2n}

Alkane anybody who doesn't learn this lot properly...

Six details and three or four structural diagrams for alkanes and alkenes, plus four extra points.
It really isn't that difficult to learn the whole page until you can scribble it down from memory.
Try doing it for five minutes: Learn, cover, scribble, check, relearn, cover, scribble, check, etc.

Reactions of Alkanes and Alkenes

Addition Reactions — _Unsaturated_ becomes _Saturated_

1) Addition reactions are when one molecule adds to another.

2) Unsaturated hydrocarbons such as alkenes can do this type of reaction because their double bond opens up to form two single bonds. Other atoms can then grab on to one of these new single bonds.

3) Addition reactions turn unsaturated alkenes into saturated compounds, as there are no more spare bonds.

4) Addition reactions are not possible with the alkanes as they do not have double bonds.

Hydrogenation — _Adding Hydrogen to an Alkene_

This reaction changes unsaturated alkenes into saturated alkanes by adding a molecule of hydrogen. The conditions needed for the reaction to take place are:

1) High temperature and pressure.   2) The presence of nickel to act as a catalyst.

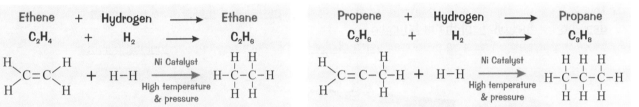

Bromination — _Adding Bromine to an Alkene_

1) Alkenes undergo an addition reaction with bromine water. This process is called bromination.

2) The bromine molecule splits and one bromine atom joins each of the carbon atoms that were joined by a double bond. The substance formed is called a saturated dibromo compound.

Example:

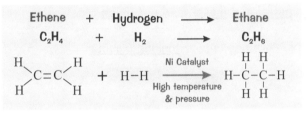

3) Bromine water is orangey brown, but the dibromo compound is colourless. So if you add bromine water to an alkene, the brown colour quickly disappears.

4) Alkanes do not react with bromine water, as they have no spare bonds for the bromine atoms to cling onto. So if you add bromine water to an alkane, the bromine stays orangey brown.

Use Bromine Water to Distinguish an Alkane from an Alkene

1) Bromine water is used to distinguish between alkanes and alkenes.
2) Bubble some of your substance through bromine water...

① ...if the colour disappears, it's an alkene. 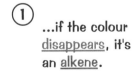 Bromine water + alkene goes colourless

② ...if the bromine remains orangey-brown, it's an alkane.  Bromine water + alkane stays brown.

Don't saturate your brain with this stuff...

Pretty dull stuff — still, you've got to learn it and learn it well for the Exam. Learn the headings, then the details for each one. And pay particularly close attention to the bromine water test to decide whether a substance is an alkane or an alkene — it's an examiners' favourite.

Cracking Hydrocarbons

Cracking — splitting up long chain hydrocarbons

1) Long chain hydrocarbons form thick gloopy liquids like tar which aren't all that useful.

2) The process called cracking turns them into shorter molecules which are much more useful.

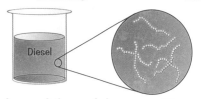 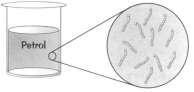

3) Cracking is a form of thermal decomposition, which just means breaking molecules down into simpler molecules by heating them.

4) A lot of the longer molecules produced from fractional distillation are cracked into smaller ones — eg. naphtha can be cracked to produce petrol.

5) This is because there's a big demand for products like petrol and diesel, and not much demand for fuel oil, naphtha or bitumen.

6) More importantly, cracking produces extra alkenes which are needed for making plastics.

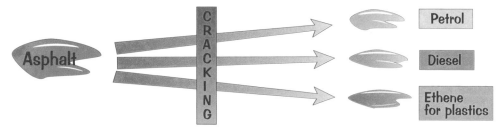

Industrial Conditions for Cracking: hot, plus a catalyst

1) Vaporised hydrocarbons are passed over powdered catalyst at about 400°C – 700°C.

2) Aluminium oxide is the catalyst used.
   The long chain molecules split apart or 'crack' on the surface of the bits of catalyst.

3) Since any of the C–C bonds can break, you usually get a mixture of products — although the conditions for the reaction are chosen so you get mostly what you want.

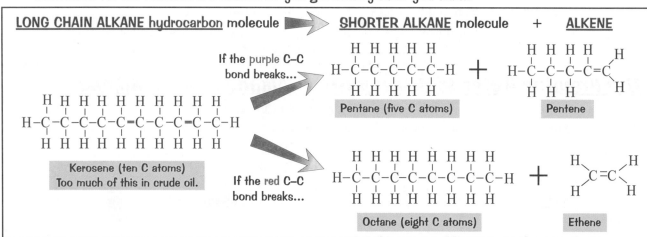

Chemistry — what a cracking subject it is...

Six details about the whys and wherefores, three details of the industrial conditions and a specific example showing typical products: a shorter chain alkane and an alkene. LEARN IT ALL.

Polymers and Plastics

Polymers and plastics were first discovered in about 1933. By 1970 it was all too late. Those halcyon days when they made *proper* motor cars with leather seats and lovely wooden dashboards were over. Sigh.

Alkenes open their double bonds to form Polymers

Under a bit of <u>pressure</u> and with a bit of a <u>catalyst</u> to help it along, many <u>small alkenes</u> will open up their <u>double bonds</u> and 'join hands' to form <u>very long chains</u> called <u>polymers</u>. There's a few things you need to know:

1) The joining up of lots of <u>individual alkenes</u> to form a <u>plastic</u> is called <u>polymerisation</u>.

2) If <u>no other products</u> are formed during the polymerisation reaction, the process is called <u>addition polymerisation</u>.

3) The <u>individual</u> units which 'join together' to form the <u>saturated polymer</u> are <u>monomers</u>.

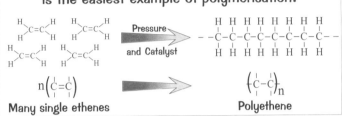

Ethene becoming <u>polyethene</u> or 'polythene' is the easiest example of polymerisation:

Pressure and Catalyst

Many single ethenes

Polyethene

There are loads of Plastics with loads of different uses

1) Polythene
1) Made from <u>ethene</u>.
2) Very <u>cheap</u> and <u>strong</u>.
3) Easily <u>moulded</u>.

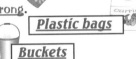

Bottles

Plastic bags

Buckets

Bowls

2) Polystyrene
1) Made from <u>styrene</u>.
2) <u>Cheap</u> and <u>easily moulded</u>.
3) Can be expanded into <u>insulating foam</u>.

Foam packaging

Radio outer cases

3) Polypropene
1) Made from <u>propene</u>.
2) Forms <u>strong fibres</u>.
3) Has <u>high elasticity</u>.

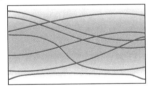
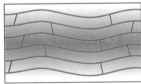

Crates

Carpets

Ropes

4) Polychloroethene (PVC)
1) Made from <u>chloroethene</u> (also called <u>vinyl chloride</u>).
2) <u>Cheap</u>.
3) Used for making <u>clothes</u> and <u>records</u>.

Records

Electric wire insulation

5) Epoxy
1) Epoxy resins are <u>polymers</u> that can be used as <u>adhesives</u>.

Intermolecular Forces Determine the Properties of Plastics

<u>Strong covalent</u> bonds hold the <u>atoms</u> together in <u>long chains</u>. But it's the bonds <u>between</u> the different molecule chains that determine the <u>properties</u> of the plastic.

Weak Intermolecular Forces:
<u>Long chains</u> held together by <u>weak intermolecular forces</u> are free to <u>slide</u> over each other. This means the plastic can be <u>stretched easily</u>, and will have a <u>low melting point</u>.

Strong Intermolecular Forces:
Plastics with <u>stronger bonds</u> between the polymer chains have <u>higher melting points</u> and <u>can't be stretched</u>, as the <u>crosslinks</u> hold the chains firmly together.

Most plastics don't rot, so they're hard to get rid of

1) Most plastics are '<u>non-biodegradable</u>' — they're not broken down by microorganisms, so they <u>don't rot</u>.
2) It's difficult to get rid of them — if you bury them in a landfill site, they'll <u>still</u> be there <u>years later</u>.
3) <u>Toxic gases</u> are given off if you <u>burn</u> plastic, so that's not a good idea either.
4) It's best to <u>recycle</u> them as this helps to conserve <u>resources</u>. Recycling is <u>expensive</u> and <u>difficult</u> though — there are lots of <u>types</u> and <u>colours</u> of plastic, and these have to be <u>separated</u> before recycling.

Revision — it's all about stringing facts together...

Learn what <u>polymerisation</u> is and practise the set of diagrams for <u>ethene</u>. Also learn all the examples given for the different types of plastics. <u>Then cover the page and scribble it all down</u>.

Revision Summary for Module CD4

This is pretty interesting stuff I reckon. Relatively speaking. Anyway, whether it is or it isn't, the only thing that really matters is whether you've learnt it all or not. These questions aren't exactly friendly, but they're a seriously serious way of finding out what you don't know. And don't forget, that's what revision is all about — finding out what you don't know and then learning it till you do. Practise these questions as often as necessary — not just once. Your ultimate aim is to be able to answer all of them easily.

1) Which kind of atoms tend to do covalent bonding?

2) Draw diagrams of the following molecules: a) H_2 b) Cl_2 c) CO_2 d) O_2
                                                   e) H_2O f) CH_4 g) C_2H_4

3) Draw a diagram showing how water and carbon dioxide are bonded.

4) How strong are the bonds between water molecules?

5) Do water and carbon dioxide have high or low boiling points? Why?

6) Do they conduct electricity? Why?

7) What are the three types of carbon?

8) How are the molecules in diamond arranged? How does this explain its physical properties?

9) How are the bonds in graphite different from diamond?

10) List the physical properties of graphite. Why does it have these properties?

11) What are hydrocarbons?

12) How can you identify a saturated compound? What about unsaturated compounds?

13) What are alkanes and alkenes? What is the basic difference between them?

14) Draw the structures of the first four alkanes and the first three alkenes and give their names.

15) List four differences in the chemical properties of alkanes and alkenes.

16) What is the general chemical formula for an alkane? What about an alkene?

17) Give a definition of an addition reaction.

18) What are the conditions needed for the addition reaction between hydrogen and an alkene? What is the name of this type of reaction?

19) What is produced when an alkene reacts with bromine water?

20) What is 'cracking'? Why is it done? What type of bonds are broken?

21) Why is it done?

22) Give a typical example of a substance which is cracked and the product(s) that you get.

23) What are the industrial conditions used for cracking?

24) What are polymers? What kind of substances can form polymers?

25) What are the small molecules used to make polymers called?

26) How are the atoms in plastics held together?

27) What are the properties of plastics which have strong intermolecular forces?

28) What about plastics with weak intermolecular forces?

29) Name four types of plastic, give their physical properties and say what they're used for.

30) How can plastics be disposed of? Which is the best method?

Chemical Equations

Equations need a lot of practice if you're going to get them right. They can get real tricky real quickly, unless you really know your stuff. Every time you do an equation you need to practise getting it right rather than skating over it.

Chemical Formulas tell you How Many Atoms there are

1) Hydrogen chloride has the chemical formula HCl. This means that in any molecule of hydrogen chloride there will be: one atom of hydrogen (H) bonded to one atom of chlorine (Cl).

2) Ammonia has the formula NH_3. This means that in any molecule of ammonia there will be: three atoms of hydrogen (H) bonded to one atom of nitrogen (N). Simple.

3) A chemical reaction can be described by the process reactants → products.

$$CH_4 + 2O_2 \rightarrow CO_2 + 2H_2O$$

ie.   methane (CH_4) reacts with oxygen (O_2) to produce carbon dioxide (CO_2) and water (H_2O).

You have to know how to write these reactions in both words and symbols, as shown below:

The Symbol Equation shows the Atoms on Both Sides:

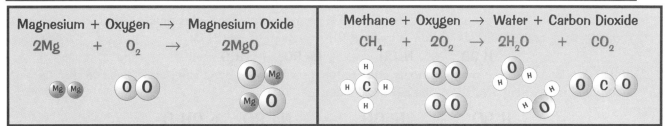

Magnesium + Oxygen → Magnesium Oxide
$$2Mg + O_2 \rightarrow 2MgO$$

Methane + Oxygen → Water + Carbon Dioxide
$$CH_4 + 2O_2 \rightarrow 2H_2O + CO_2$$

You need to know how to write out any Equation...

You really do need to know how to write out chemical equations. In fact, you need to know how to write out equations for pretty well all the reactions in this book.
That might sound like an awful lot, but there aren't nearly as many as you think. Have a look.
You also need to know the formulae for all the ionic and covalent compounds in here too. Lovely.

State Symbols tell you what Physical State it's in

These are easy enough, just make sure you know them, especially aq (aqueous).

(s) — Solid	(l) — Liquid	(g) — Gas	(aq) — Dissolved in water

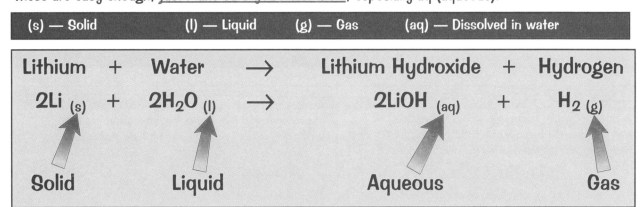

Lithium + Water → Lithium Hydroxide + Hydrogen
$$2Li_{(s)} + 2H_2O_{(l)} \rightarrow 2LiOH_{(aq)} + H_{2(g)}$$

Solid   Liquid   Aqueous   Gas

It's tricky — but don't get yourself in a state over it...

Make sure you know the formulae for all the ionic and covalent compounds you've come across so far. Try writing symbol equations for the following equations and put the state symbols in too: 1) Iron(III) oxide + hydrogen → iron + water   (Answers on p. 104)
   2) Hydrochloric acid + aluminium → aluminium chloride + hydrogen

Balancing Equations

Balancing The Equation — match them up one by one

1) There must always be the <u>same</u> number of atoms on <u>both sides</u>, they can't just <u>disappear</u>.

2) You <u>balance</u> the equation by putting numbers <u>in front</u> of the formulae where needed.

   Take this equation for reacting sulphuric acid with sodium hydroxide:

$$H_2SO_4 \ + \ NaOH \ \rightarrow \ Na_2SO_4 + H_2O \quad \Longleftarrow \quad \underset{\text{balanced.}}{\overset{\text{Not}}{}}$$

The <u>formulae</u> are all correct but the numbers of some atoms <u>don't match up</u> on both sides.
You <u>can't change formulae</u> like H_2SO_4 to H_2SO_5. You can only put numbers <u>in front of them</u>:

Method: Balance just ONE type of atom at a time

The more you practise, the quicker you get, but all you do is this:

> 1) Find an element that <u>*doesn't balance*</u> and <u>*pencil in a number*</u> to try and sort it out.
> 2) <u>*See where it gets you.*</u> It may create <u>*another imbalance*</u> but pencil in <u>*another number*</u>
>   and see where that gets you.
> 3) Carry on chasing <u>*unbalanced*</u> elements and it'll <u>*sort itself out*</u> pretty quickly.

In the equation above you soon notice we're short of H atoms on the right hand side.

1) The only thing you can do about that is make it $2H_2O$ instead of just H_2O:

$$H_2SO_4 \ + \ NaOH \ \rightarrow \ Na_2SO_4 + 2H_2O$$

2) But that now causes too many H atoms and O atoms on the right hand side, so to balance that up
   you could try putting $2NaOH$ on the left hand side:

$$H_2SO_4 \ + \ 2NaOH \ \rightarrow \ Na_2SO_4 + 2H_2O$$

3) And suddenly there it is! <u>Everything balances</u>. And you'll notice the Na just sorted itself out.

You Need to Know these Chemical Formulae

Before you can balance anything, you need to be able to write down the right <u>chemical formulae</u>.
That means you have to <u>learn the stuff in this table</u> and how to use it.
The main thing to remember is that in compounds the <u>total charge must always add up to zero</u>.

Common Substances				Positive Ions				Negative Ions			
Hydrochloric acid	HCl	Water	H_2O	Sodium	Na^+	Copper	Cu^{2+}	Chloride	Cl^-	Sulphate	SO_4^{2-}
Nitric acid	HNO_3	Carbon dioxide	CO_2	Potassium	K^+	Iron (II)	Fe^{2+}	Hydroxide	OH^-	Oxide	O^{2-}
Sulphuric acid	H_2SO_4	Hydrogen	H_2	Calcium	Ca^{2+}	Zinc	Zn^{2+}	Nitrate	NO_3^-	Carbonate	CO_3^{2-}
Ammonia	NH_3	Oxygen	O_2	Magnesium	Mg^{2+}						

<u>EXAMPLE</u>: Find the formula for <u>zinc nitrate</u>.

A zinc ion has a +2 charge and a nitrate ion has
a –1 charge. To balance the total charge you
need two nitrate ions for every one zinc ion.

$$Zn(NO_3)_2$$

Put the NO_3 in brackets, otherwise NO_{32}
would look like you mean 32 oxygen atoms.

<u>EXAMPLE</u>: The formula for <u>potassium sulphate</u>.

A potassium ion is K^+ and a sulphate ion is SO_4^{2-}.
So the formula of potassium sulphate must be:

$$K_2SO_4$$

You need two K^+ ions to balance
the charge on the SO_4^{2-} ion.

This revision lark —it's all a balancing act...

Learning how to balance chemical equations is <u>really</u> important. Unfortunately, the only way to get any good
at it is to <u>practise, practise, practise</u> So balance the equation below and name the substances involved:

$$H_2 \ + \ O_2 \ \rightarrow \ H_2O$$

Relative Formula Mass

The biggest trouble with <u>Relative atomic mass</u> and <u>Relative formula mass</u> is that they <u>sound</u> so bloodcurdling. In fact, they're dead easy. Take a few deep breaths, and just enjoy, as the mists slowly clear...

Relative Atomic Mass, A_r — *easy peasy*

1) This is just a way of saying how <u>heavy</u> different atoms are <u>compared with each other</u>.
2) The <u>relative atomic mass</u> A_r is nothing more than the <u>mass number</u> of the element.
3) In the Periodic Table, the elements all have <u>two</u> numbers. The smaller one is the atomic number (how many protons it has). But the <u>bigger one</u> is the <u>mass number</u> (how many protons and neutrons it has) which, kind of obviously, is also the <u>relative atomic mass</u>. Easy peasy, I'd say.

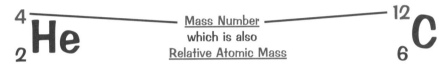

$$^4_2\text{He} \qquad \text{Mass Number which is also Relative Atomic Mass} \qquad ^{12}_6\text{C}$$

Helium has A_r = 4. Carbon has A_r = 12. (So carbon atoms are <u>3 times heavier</u> than helium atoms.)

Relative Formula Mass, M_r — *also easy peasy*

If you have a compound like $MgCl_2$ then it has a <u>relative formula mass</u>, M_r, which is just all the relative atomic masses <u>added together</u>.

For $MgCl_2$ it would be:

$$\text{MgCl}_2$$
$$24 + (35.5 \times 2) = 95$$

> So the M_r for $MgCl_2$ is simply <u>95</u>

You can easily get the A_r for any element from the <u>Periodic Table</u> (see inside front cover), but in a lot of questions they give you them anyway.

I'll tell you what, since it's nearly Christmas I'll run through another couple of examples.

Compounds with Brackets in...

> *Find the relative formula mass for calcium hydroxide, $Ca(OH)_2$*

<u>ANSWER:</u> The <u>small number 2</u> after the bracket in the formula $Ca(OH)_2$ means that <u>there's two of everything inside the brackets</u>. But that doesn't make the question any harder really.

> The brackets in the sum are in the same place as the brackets in the chemical formula

$$\text{Ca(OH)}_2$$
$$40 + (16 + 1) \times 2 = 74$$

> So the Relative Formula Mass for $Ca(OH)_2$ is <u>74</u>

Hydrates — Compounds combined with Water

Some compounds combine with <u>water</u> to form <u>hydrates</u>. For example, <u>hydrated copper (II) sulphate</u> has the formula $CuSO_4.5H_2O$, which means 5 water molecules are joined to every copper (II) sulphate particle.

> *Find the relative formula mass of hydrated copper (II) sulphate.*

> Put a '+' sign in the sum in place of the 'dot' in the chemical formula

$$\text{CuSO}_4 . 5\text{H}_2\text{O}$$
$$160 + (5 \times 18) \quad \text{(Check it)}$$

> So the M_r for $CuSO_4.5H_2O$ is <u>250</u>

Phew, Chemistry — scary stuff sometimes, innit...

When you know it, <u>cover the page</u> and <u>scribble down</u> the important details. D'ya miss any?
1) Use the Periodic Table to find the relative atomic mass of these elements: Cu, K, Kr, Fe, Cl.
2) Find the relative formula mass of these compounds: NaOH, $Mg(NO_3)_2$, $FeCl_3.6H_2O$.

Empirical Formula

Although Relative Atomic Mass and Relative Formula Mass are easy enough, it can get just a tadge trickier when you start getting into other calculations which use them. It depends on how good your maths is basically, because it's all to do with ratios and percentages.

Finding The Empirical Formula (from Experimental Masses)

This also sounds a lot worse than it really is. Try this for an easy peasy stepwise method:

> 1) *LIST ALL THE ELEMENTS* in the compound (there's usually only two or three!).
> 2) *Underneath them*, write their *EXPERIMENTAL MASSES OR PERCENTAGES*.
> 3) *DIVIDE* each mass or percentage *BY THE A_r* for that particular element.
> 4) Turn the numbers you get into *A NICE SIMPLE RATIO*
>   by multiplying and/or dividing them by well-chosen numbers.
> 5) Get the ratio in its *SIMPLEST FORM*, and that tells you the formula of the compound.

Example 1: *Find the empirical formula of the iron oxide produced when 44.8g of iron react with 19.2g of oxygen. (A_r for iron = 56, A_r for oxygen =16)*

Method:

1) List the two elements:	Fe	O
2) Write in the experimental masses:	44.8	19.2
3) Divide by the A_r for each element:	$44.8/56 = 0.8$	$19.2/16 = 1.2$
4) Multiply by 10...	8	12
...then divide by 4:	2	3

5) So the simplest formula is 2 atoms of Fe to 3 atoms of O, ie. Fe_2O_3. And that's it done.

If you're given Percentages — just pretend you've got 100g

Example 2: *Find the empirical formula of a compound whose mass is made up of 80% carbon and 20% hydrogen. (A_r for carbon = 12, A_r for hydrogen =1)*

If you only know the percentages of the elements in the compound, but not the actual masses from an experiment, just assume you've got 100g of the compound. Then use the above method.

Method:

1) List the two elements:	C	H
2) Write in the experimental masses:	80	20
3) Divide by the A_r for each element:	$80/12 = 6.67$	$20/1 = 20$
4) Multiply by 3...	20	60
...then divide by 20	1	3

The molecular formula could be C_2H_6, but the empirical formulae is always the simplest possible ratio.

5) So the simplest formula is 1 atom of carbon to 3 atoms of hydrogen, ie. CH_3.

> *You need to realise (for the Exam) that this empirical method (ie. based on experiment) is the only way of finding out the formula of a compound. Rust is iron oxide, sure, but is it FeO, or Fe_2O_3? Only an experiment to determine the empirical formula will tell you for certain.*

Old Dmitri Mendeleyev did this sort of thing in his sleep — the old rogue...

Make sure you learn the five rules in the reddish-brown box at the top. Then try these:
1) Find the empirical formula when 3.25g of zinc (Zn) reacts with 3.55g of chlorine (Cl).
2) Find the empirical formula of a compound made up of 75% carbon and 25% hydrogen.

Calculating Masses in Reactions

These can be kinda scary too, but chill out, little white-faced one — just relax and enjoy.

The Three Important Steps — not to be missed...

(Miss one out and it'll all go horribly wrong, believe me.)

1) *WRITE OUT* the balanced *EQUATION*
2) *Work out* M_r — just for the *TWO BITS YOU WANT*
3) Apply the rule: *DIVIDE TO GET ONE, THEN MULTIPLY TO GET ALL*
   (But you have to apply this first to the substance they give information about, and *then* the other one!)

EXAMPLE: *What mass of magnesium oxide is produced when 60g of magnesium is burned in air?*

ANSWER:

1) Write out the <u>BALANCED EQUATION</u>:

$$2Mg + O_2 \rightarrow 2MgO$$

2) Work out the <u>RELATIVE FORMULA MASSES</u>:

(don't do the oxygen — we don't need it)

$$2 \times 24 \qquad \rightarrow 2 \times (24+16)$$
$$48 \qquad \rightarrow \qquad 80$$

3) Apply the rule: <u>DIVIDE TO GET ONE, THEN MULTIPLY TO GET ALL</u>.
   The two numbers, 48 and 80, tell us that   *48g of Mg react to give 80g of MgO.*
   You've now got to be able to write this down:

> 48g of Mg ...... reacts to give ..... 80g of MgO
>
> 1g of Mg ...... reacts to give .....
>
> 60g of Mg ...... reacts to give ......

<u>The big clue</u> is that in the question they've said we want to burn "<u>60g of magnesium</u>".
ie. they've told us how much <u>magnesium</u> to have, and that's how you know to write down the <u>left hand side</u> of it first, because:

We'll first need to ÷ by 48 to get 1g of Mg
and then need to × by 60 to get 60g of Mg.

<u>Then</u> you can work out the numbers on the other side (shown in orange below) by realising that you must <u>divide both sides by 48</u> and then <u>multiply both sides by 60</u>. It's tricky.

÷48 {
48g of Mg .... 80g of MgO
1g of Mg .... 1.67g of MgO
60g of Mg .... 100g of MgO
} ÷48
×60   ×60

You should realise that <u>in practice</u> 100% yield may not be obtained in some reactions, so the amount of product might be <u>slightly less than calculated</u>.

This finally tells us that <u>60g of magnesium will produce 100g of magnesium oxide</u>.

If the question had said "Find how much magnesium gives 500g of magnesium oxide.", you'd fill in the MgO side first instead, <u>because that's the one you'd have the information about</u>.   Got it? Good-O!

Reaction Mass Calculations? — no worries, matey...

<u>Learn the three rules</u> in the red box and practise the example till you can do it fluently.
1) Find the mass of calcium which gives 30g of calcium oxide (CaO), when burnt in air.
2) Find the mass of sodium oxide (Na_2O) made when 69g of sodium is burnt in air.

The Mole

The Mole is really confusing. I think it's the word that puts people off. It's very difficult to see the relevance of the word "mole" to different-sized piles of brightly-coloured powders.

"THE MOLE" is simply the name given to a certain number

Just like "a million" is this many: 1 000 000; or "a billion" is this many: 1 000 000 000,
so "a mole" is this many: 602 300 000 000 000 000 000 000 or 6.023×10^{23}.

1) And that's all it is. Just a number. The burning question, of course, is why is it such a silly long one like that, and with a six at the front?

2) The answer is that when you get precisely that number of atoms or molecules, of any element or compound, then, conveniently, they weigh exactly the same number of grams as the Relative Atomic Mass, A_r (or M_r) of the element or compound.
This is arranged on purpose of course, to make things easier.

> One mole of atoms or molecules of any substance will have a mass in grams
> equal to the Relative Formula Mass (A_r or M_r) for that substance.

EXAMPLES:
Carbon has an A_r of 12.   So one mole of carbon weighs exactly 12g
Iron has an A_r of 56.   So one mole of iron weighs exactly 56g
Nitrogen gas, N_2, has an M_r of 28 ($= 2 \times 14$).   So one mole of N_2 weighs exactly 28g
Carbon dioxide, CO_2, has an M_r of 44.   So one mole of CO_2 weighs exactly 44g

This means that 12g of carbon, or 56g of iron, or 28g of N_2, or 44g of CO_2, all contain the same number of particles, namely one mole or 6.023×10^{23} atoms or molecules.

Nice Easy Formula for finding the Number of Moles in a given mass:

$$\text{NUMBER OF MOLES} = \frac{\text{Mass in g} \quad \text{(of element or compound)}}{M_r \quad \text{(of element or compound)}}$$

EXAMPLE: How many moles are there in 42g of carbon?
ANSWER: No. of moles = Mass (g) / M_r = 42/12 = 3.5 moles   Easy Peasy

"Relative Formula Mass" is also "Molar Mass"

1) We've been very happy using the Relative Formula Mass, M_r, all through the calculations.

2) In fact, that was already using the idea of Moles because M_r is actually the mass of one mole in g, or as we sometimes call it, the MOLAR MASS.

A "One Molar Solution" Contains "One Mole per Litre"

...and so, for example, a 2M (ie. 2 molar) solution of NaOH contains 2 moles per litre of solution. Easy really. You'll need this formula to find the number of moles in a given volume:

$$\text{NUMBER OF MOLES} = \text{VOLUME in Litres} \times \text{MOLARITY of solution}$$

EXAMPLE: How many moles in 185cm³ of a 2M solution?   ANS: $0.185 \times 2 = 0.37$ moles

Moles — a suitably silly name for such a confusing idea...

It's possible to do all the calculations on the previous pages without ever talking about moles. You just concentrate on M_r and A_r all the time instead. In fact M_r and A_r represent moles anyway, but I think it's less confusing if moles aren't mentioned at all. But you need to learn this page anyway, as it's vital stuff.

Percentage Yield

Percentage yield tells you about the <u>overall success</u> of an experiment. It compares what you think you should get (<u>predicted yield</u>) with what you get in practice (<u>actual yield</u>).

Percentage Yield Compares Actual and Predicted Yield

The more reactants you start with, the higher the <u>actual yield</u> will be — that's pretty obvious. But the <u>percentage yield</u> tells you what <u>proportion</u> of the original reactants have been converted into product. It <u>doesn't</u> depend on the amount of reactants you started with — it's a <u>percentage</u>.

1) The <u>predicted yield</u> of a reaction can be calculated from the <u>balanced reaction equation</u> (see page 46).

2) Percentage yield is given by the formula:

$$\text{percentage yield} = \frac{\text{actual yield (grams)}}{\text{predicted yield (grams)}} \times 100$$

3) Percentage yield is <u>always</u> somewhere between 0 and 100%.

4) A 100% yield means that <u>all</u> the reactants were converted into product.

5) A 0% yield means that <u>no</u> reactants were converted into product, ie. no product at all was <u>made</u>.

Yields are always Less Than 100%

In real life, you <u>never</u> get a 100% yield. Some product or reactant <u>always</u> gets lost along the way — and that goes for big <u>industrial processes</u> as well as school lab experiments. How this happens depends on <u>what sort of reaction</u> it is and what <u>apparatus</u> is being used.

Lots of things can go wrong, but the four you need to <u>know about</u> are:

1) Evaporation

Liquids evaporate <u>all the time</u> — not just while they're being heated.

Liquid evaporating...

2) Heating

Losses while heating can be due to <u>evaporation</u>, or for more complicated reasons.

In <u>reversible reactions</u>, increasing the temperature moves the <u>equilibrium position</u>.

So heating the reaction to speed it up might mean a <u>lower yield</u>.

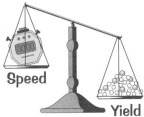
Speed
Yield

3) Filtration

When you <u>filter a liquid</u> to remove <u>solid particles</u>, you nearly always lose a bit of liquid or a bit of solid.

1) If you want to <u>keep the liquid</u>, you lose the bit that remains with the solid and filter paper (as they always stay a bit wet).

2) If you want to <u>keep the solid</u>, some of it usually gets left behind when you scrape it off the filter paper — even if you're really careful.

4) Transferring Liquids

You always lose a bit of liquid when you <u>transfer</u> it from one container to another — even if you manage not to spill it.

Some of it always gets left behind on the <u>inside surface</u> of the old container. Think about it — it's always wet when you finish.

You can't always get what you want...

The formula for <u>yield</u> is almost certain to be in the Exam, so make sure you can write it down without even thinking. Then learn the <u>four sections</u> in the second bit, cover the page and scribble down the main points under each heading. Keep doing it until you can do it <u>perfectly</u>.

Reversible Reactions in Equilibrium

A <u>reversible reaction</u> is one where the <u>products</u> of a reaction can react with each other and <u>convert back</u> to the original reactants. In other words, <u>it can go both ways</u>.

> A <u>REVERSIBLE REACTION</u> IS ONE WHERE THE <u>PRODUCTS</u> OF THE REACTION CAN <u>THEMSELVES REACT</u> TO PRODUCE THE <u>ORIGINAL REACTANTS</u>
>
> A + B ⇌ C + D

Reversible Reactions will reach Dynamic Equilibrium

1) If a reversible reaction takes place in a <u>closed system</u> then a state of <u>equilibrium</u> will always be reached.

2) <u>Equilibrium</u> means that the <u>relative (%) quantities</u> of reactants and products will reach a certain <u>balance</u> and stay there. "<u>A closed system</u>" just means that none of the reactants or products can <u>escape</u>.

3) It is in fact a <u>DYNAMIC EQUILIBRIUM</u>, which means that the reactions are still taking place <u>in both directions</u> but the overall effect is <u>nil</u>, because the forward and reverse reactions <u>cancel each other out</u>. The reactions are taking place at <u>exactly the same rate</u> in both directions.

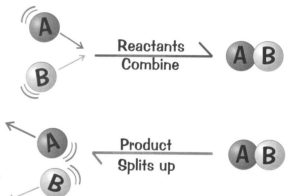

Reactants Combine

Product Splits up

Dynamic Equilibrium

Changing Temperature and Pressure to get More Product

1) In a reversible reaction the "<u>position of equilibrium</u>" (the <u>relative amounts</u> of reactants and products) depends <u>very strongly</u> on the <u>temperature</u> and <u>pressure</u> surrounding the reaction.

2) If we <u>deliberately alter</u> the temperature and pressure we can <u>move</u> the "position of equilibrium" to give <u>more product</u> and <u>less</u> reactants.

Two very simple rules for which way the equilibrium will move

1) All reactions <u>give out heat</u> in one direction (ie. they're <u>exothermic</u>) and <u>take in heat</u> in the other (ie. they're <u>endothermic</u>).
If we <u>raise the temperature</u>, the <u>endothermic</u> reaction will increase to <u>use up</u> the extra heat.
If we <u>reduce the temperature</u> the <u>exothermic</u> reaction will increase to <u>give out</u> more heat.

2) Many reactions have a <u>greater volume</u> on one side, either of <u>products</u> or <u>reactants</u>.
If we <u>raise the pressure</u> it will encourage the reaction which produces <u>less volume</u>.
If we <u>lower the pressure</u> it will encourage the reaction which produces <u>more volume</u>.

This is all summed up very nicely by the principle which states:

> IF YOU <u>CHANGE THE CONDITIONS</u>, THE <u>POSITION OF EQUILIBRIUM</u> WILL <u>SHIFT</u> TO <u>OPPOSE</u> THE CHANGE

This is called <u>Le Chatelier's Principle</u> — but you don't need to know the name

Learning/forgetting— the worst reversible of them all...

I reckon reversible reactions are easy to understand — they get together, they split up, get together, split up... familiar story? Anyway, there's three sections here: the definition of a reversible reaction, the notion of a dynamic equilibrium and the principle at the bottom of the page — <u>learn it all</u>.

The Haber Process

This is an <u>important industrial process</u>. It produces <u>ammonia</u> (NH_3), which is needed for making <u>fertilisers</u>.

The Haber Process is a Reversible Reaction:

$$N_{2\,(g)} \quad + \quad 3H_{2\,(g)} \quad \rightleftharpoons \quad 2NH_{3\,(g)} \quad (+ \text{ heat})$$

1) The <u>nitrogen</u> is obtained easily from the <u>air</u>, which is <u>78% nitrogen</u> (and 21% oxygen).
2) You don't need to know where the hydrogen comes from, so <u>don't worry</u> about it.
3) Because the reaction is <u>reversible</u>, not all of the nitrogen and hydrogen will <u>convert</u> to ammonia. The reaction reaches a <u>dynamic equilibrium</u>.
4) The N_2 and H_2 which don't react are <u>recycled</u> and passed through again so <u>none is wasted</u>.

Industrial conditions:
PRESSURE: 200 atmospheres;   **TEMPERATURE**: 450°C;   **CATALYST**: Iron

Because the Reaction is Reversible, there's a Compromise to be made:

1) <u>Higher pressures</u> favour the <u>forward</u> reaction (since there are four moles of gas on the left hand side, but only two moles on the right).

2) So the pressure is set <u>as high as possible</u> to give the best % yield, without making the plant too expensive to build (it'd be too expensive to build a plant that'd stand pressures of over 1000 atmospheres, for example). Hence the <u>200 atmospheres</u> operating pressure.

3) The <u>forward reaction</u> is <u>exothermic</u>, which means that <u>increasing</u> the <u>temperature</u> will actually move the equilibrium the <u>wrong way</u> — away from ammonia and towards N_2 and H_2.
So the yield of ammonia would be greater at <u>lower temperatures</u>.

4) The trouble is, <u>lower temperatures</u> mean a <u>slower rate of reaction</u>. So what they do is increase the temperature anyway, to get a much faster rate of reaction.

5) The 450°C is a <u>compromise</u> between <u>maximum yield</u> and <u>speed of reaction</u>. It's better to wait just <u>20 seconds</u> for a <u>10% yield</u> than to have to wait <u>60 seconds</u> for a <u>20% yield</u>.

6) Remember, the unused hydrogen, H_2, and nitrogen, N_2, are <u>recycled</u> so <u>nothing is wasted</u>.

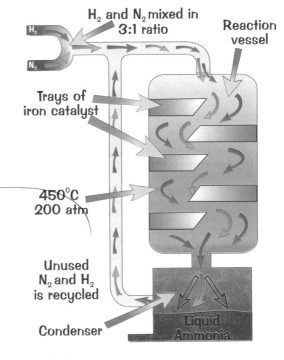

H_2 and N_2 mixed in 3:1 ratio

Reaction vessel

Trays of iron catalyst

450°C 200 atm

Unused N_2 and H_2 is recycled

Condenser

Liquid Ammonia

The Iron Catalyst Speeds up the Reaction and Keeps Costs Down

1) The <u>iron catalyst</u> makes the reaction go <u>faster</u> which gets it to the <u>equilibrium proportions</u> more quickly. But remember, the catalyst <u>doesn't</u> affect the <u>position</u> of equilibrium (ie. the % yield).

2) <u>Without the catalyst</u> the temperature would have to be <u>raised even further</u> to get a <u>quick enough</u> reaction and that would <u>reduce the % yield</u> even further. So the catalyst is very important.

200 atmospheres? — that could give you a headache..

There are quite a lot of details on this page. They're pretty keen on the Haber process in the Exams so you'd be well advised to learn all this. They could easily ask you about any of these details. Use the same good old method: <u>Learn it, cover it up, repeat it back to yourself, check, try again...</u>

Minimising the Cost of Production

Things like <u>fast reaction rates</u> and <u>high % yields</u> are nice in industry — but in the end, the important thing is <u>keeping costs down</u>. It all comes down to maximum efficiency...

Production Cost Depends on Several Different Factors

There are <u>five</u> main things that affect the <u>cost</u> of making a new substance. It's these five factors that companies have to consider when deciding <u>if</u>, and then <u>how</u>, to produce a chemical.

1) Price of Energy

a) Industry needs to keep its <u>energy bills</u> as low as possible.

b) If a reaction needs a <u>high temperature</u>, the <u>running costs</u> will be higher.

2) Cost of Raw Materials

a) This is kept to a minimum by <u>recycling</u> any <u>materials</u> that haven't reacted.

b) A good example of this is the <u>Haber Process</u>. The % yield of the reaction is quite <u>low</u> (about 10%), but the unreacted N_2 and H_2 can be <u>recycled</u> to keep waste to a minimum.

3) Labour Costs (Wages)

a) Everyone who works for a company has got to be <u>paid</u>.

b) <u>Labour intensive</u> processes (ie. those that involve many people), can be very expensive.

c) <u>Automation</u> cuts <u>running costs</u> by reducing the number of people involved.

d) But companies have always got to weigh any <u>savings</u> they make on their <u>wage bill</u> against the <u>initial cost</u> of the machinery.

4) Plant Costs (Equipment)

a) The cost of equipment depends on the <u>conditions</u> it has to cope with.

b) For example, it costs far more to make something to withstand <u>very high pressures</u> than something which only needs to work at one atmosphere.

5) Rate of Production

a) Generally speaking, the faster the reaction goes, the better it is in terms of reducing the time and costs of production.

b) So rates of reaction are often increased by using <u>catalysts</u>.

c) But the increase in production rate has to <u>balance the cost</u> of buying the catalyst in the first place.

Optimum Conditions are chosen to give the Lowest Cost

1) Optimum conditions are those that give the <u>lowest production cost</u> — even if this means compromising on the <u>speed of reaction</u> or <u>% yield</u>. Learn the definition.

> OPTIMUM CONDITIONS are those that give the LOWEST PRODUCTION COST

2) However, the <u>rate of reaction</u> and <u>percentage yield</u> must both be <u>high enough</u> to make a <u>sufficient amount</u> of product each day.

3) Don't forget, a <u>low percentage yield is okay</u>, as long as the starting materials can be recycled.

Faster, better, cheaper — kerplunk...

The <u>Haber Process</u> is a brilliant example of pretty much all the stuff on this page. You need to learn those <u>five</u> different factors affecting cost, and the definition of '<u>optimum conditions</u>'. <u>Cover</u> the page and <u>scribble</u> it all down. And keep doing it until you get it <u>all</u> right.

Higher *Higher* *Higher* *Higher*

Acids and Bases

The pH Scale and Universal Indicator

pH 1 2 3 4 5 6 7 8 9 10 11 12 13 14

← ACIDS — NEUTRAL — ALKALIS →

car battery acid, stomach acid | vinegar, lemon juice | acid rain | normal rain | tap water, milk | washing up liquid | pancreatic juice | soap powder | ammonia

The pH scale goes from 1 to 14.

1) The strongest acid has pH 1. The strongest alkali has pH 14.

2) A neutral substance has pH 7 (eg. pure water).

3) An indicator is a dye that changes colour, depending on whether it's in an acid or an alkali.
Universal indicator is a very useful combination of dyes which gives the colours shown above.

Acids and Bases Neutralise Each Other

An ACID is a substance with a pH of less than 7. Acids form $H^+_{(aq)}$ ions in water.
A BASE is a substance with a pH of greater than 7.
An ALKALI is a base that DISSOLVES IN WATER. Alkalis form $OH^-_{(aq)}$ ions in water.

The reaction between acids and bases is called neutralisation. Make sure you learn it:

$$acid + base \rightarrow salt + water$$

Neutralisation can also be seen in terms of H^+ and OH^- ions like this, so learn it too:

$$H^+_{(aq)} + OH^-_{(aq)} \rightarrow H_2O_{(l)}$$

When an acid neutralises a base (or vice versa), the products are neutral, ie. they have a pH of 7.

Three "Real life" Examples of Neutralisation:

1) Indigestion is caused by too much hydrochloric acid in the stomach.
Indigestion tablets contain alkalis such as magnesium oxide, which neutralise the excess HCl.

2) Fields with acidic soils can be improved no end by adding lime.
The lime added to fields is calcium hydroxide $Ca(OH)_2$, which is of course an alkali.

3) Lakes affected by acid rain can also be neutralised by adding lime. This saves the fish.

Hydrochloric acid produces Chlorides

$HCl + NaOH \rightarrow NaCl + H_2O$ (Sodium chloride)
$2HCl + CuO \rightarrow CuCl_2 + H_2O$ (Copper chloride)

Hydrochloric acid and sulphuric acid also produce chlorides and sulphates when they react with metals.

Sulphuric acid produces Sulphates

$H_2SO_4 + 2KOH \rightarrow K_2SO_4 + 2H_2O$ (Potassium sulphate)
$H_2SO_4 + CuO \rightarrow CuSO_4 + H_2O$ (Copper sulphate)

Nitric acid produces Nitrates when neutralised by Alkalis

$HNO_3 + NaOH \rightarrow NaNO_3 + H_2O$ (Sodium nitrate)
$2HNO_3 + Cu(OH)_2 \rightarrow Cu(NO_3)_2 + 2H_2O$ (Copper nitrate)

But nitric acid plays silly devils when it reacts with metals and produces nitrogen oxides instead.

Higher

Hey man, like "acid", yeah — eeuuucch...

Try and enjoy this page on acids and bases, because it gets really tedious from now on. These are very basic facts and possibly quite interesting. Cover the page and scribble them down.

Fertilisers

On this page are two reactions involving ammonia you need to be familiar with, along with some stuff about fertilisers. Somehow, I don't think I'd have any of this on my list of "Top Ten Most Riveting Chemistry Topics".

Fertilisers Provide Plants with the Essential Elements for Growth

1) The three main essential elements in fertilisers are nitrogen, phosphorus and potassium. If plants don't get enough of these elements, their growth and life processes are affected. For example, nitrogen is used to make plant proteins, which are essential for growth.

2) Sometimes these elements are missing from the soil because they've been used up by a previous crop.

3) Fertilisers replace these missing elements or provide more of them. This helps to increase the crop yield.

4) It's essential that water is present if fertilisers are to be effective. This is because the fertiliser must first dissolve in water before it can be taken in by the crop roots.

Ammonia can be Neutralised with Acids to Produce Fertilisers

1) Ammonia is an alkali, and can be neutralised by acids to make ammonium salts.

2) Ammonium nitrate is an especially good fertiliser because it has nitrogen from two sources, the ammonia and the nitric acid. Kind of a double dose.

$$NH_{3\,(g)} + HNO_{3\,(aq)} \rightarrow NH_4NO_{3\,(aq)}$$
Ammonia + Nitric acid → Ammonium nitrate

These are neutralisation reactions, but using ammonia as the base you only get an ammonium salt — not salt + water.

3) Ammonium sulphate can also be used as a fertiliser, and is made by neutralising sulphuric acid with ammonia:

$$2NH_{3\,(g)} + H_2SO_{4\,(aq)} \rightarrow (NH_4)_2SO_{4\,(aq)}$$
Ammonia + Sulphuric acid → Ammonium sulphate

4) Two other fertilisers manufactured using ammonia are ammonium phosphate and urea.

Fertilisers Damage Lakes and Rivers — Eutrophication

1) Fertilisers which contain nitrates are essential to modern farming.

2) But you get problems if some of the rich fertiliser finds its way into rivers and streams.

3) This happens quite easily if too much fertiliser is applied, especially if it rains soon afterwards.

4) The result is EUTROPHICATION, which basically means "too much of a good thing". (Raw sewage pumped into rivers can cause the same problem.)

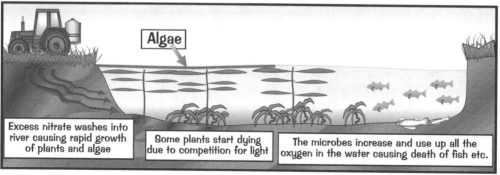

Algae

Excess nitrate washes into river causing rapid growth of plants and algae

Some plants start dying due to competition for light

The microbes increase and use up all the oxygen in the water causing death of fish etc.

As the picture shows, too many nitrates in the water cause a sequence of "mega-growth", "mega-death" and "mega-decay" involving most of the plant and animal life in the water.

5) Farmers need to take a lot more care when spreading artificial fertilisers.

Using urea as a fertiliser — you must be taking the...

Make sure you know all the points on this page about fertilisers and eutrophication, as well as the diagram. You know the drill, learn them, cover the page and try and scribble it all down. And if you make any mistakes... learn it again, cover it again, and scribble it all down again.

Revision Summary for Module CD5

Some more horrid questions to stress you out. The thing is though, why bother doing easy questions? These meaty monsters find out what you really know, and worse, what you really don't. Yeah, I know, it's kinda scary, but if you want to get anywhere in life you've got to face up to a bit of hardship. That's just the way it is. Take a few deep breaths and then try these...

1) Give three rules for balancing equations. Balance these and put the state symbols in:
   a) $CaCO_3 + HCl \rightarrow CaCl_2 + H_2O + CO_2$
   b) $Ca + H_2O \rightarrow Ca(OH)_2 + H_2$
   c) $H_2SO_4 + KOH \rightarrow K_2SO_4 + H_2O$
   d) $Fe_2O_3 + H_2 \rightarrow Fe + H_2O$

2) What are A_r and M_r?

3) What is the relationship between A_r and the number of protons and neutrons in the atom?

4) Find A_r or M_r for these (use the Periodic Table inside the front cover):
   a) Ca   b) Ag   c) CO_2 d) $MgCO_3$ e) $AlCl_3.6H_2O$
   f) ZnO   g) Na_2CO_3 h) sodium chloride

5) What is meant by an empirical formula (EF)?

6) Work these out (using the Periodic Table):
   a) Find the EF for the iron oxide formed when 45.1g of iron reacts with 19.3g of oxygen.
   b) Find the EF for the compound formed when 227g of calcium reacts with 216g of fluorine.
   c) Find the EF for when 208.4g of carbon reacts with 41.7g of hydrogen.
   d) Find the EF when 21.9g of magnesium, 29.3g of sulphur and 58.4g of oxygen react.

7) Write down the three steps of the method for calculating reacting masses.
   a) What mass of magnesium oxide is produced when 112.1g of magnesium burns in air?
   b) What mass of sodium is needed to produce 108.2g of sodium oxide?
   c) What mass of carbon will react with hydrogen to produce 24.6g of propane?

8) What is a mole? Why is it that precise number? Why does it have such a silly name?

9) How much does one mole of any compound weigh? What is meant by molar mass?

10) What is the formula for percentage yield? How does percentage yield differ from actual yield?

11) Name four factors that prevent the percentage yield from being 100%.

12) What is a reversible reaction?

13) Explain what is meant by dynamic equilibrium in a reversible reaction.

14) How does changing the temperature and pressure of a reaction alter the equilibrium?

15) How does this influence the choice of pressure for the Haber Process?

16) What determines the choice of operating temperature for the Haber process?

17) What effect does the catalyst have on the reaction?

18) Where is the nitrogen needed for the Haber process obtained from?

19) Describe five factors that affect the cost of making chemicals in industry.

20) How can the cost of raw materials be kept as low as possible?

21) In industry, how are the 'optimum conditions' for a process decided?

22) Describe fully the colour of universal indicator for every pH value from 1 to 14.

23) Is the pH of nitric acid less than or greater than 7? What about the pH of ammonia?

24) What are acids and bases? What is an alkali?

25) What type of ions are always present when a) acids and b) alkalis dissolve in water?

26) Write the equation of a neutralisation reaction in terms of these ions.

27) What type of salts do a) hydrochloric acid and b) sulphuric acid produce?

28) Name three essential elements in fertilisers?

29) How does nitrogen increase the growth of plants?

30) Name two fertilisers which are manufactured from ammonia.

31) What can happen if too much fertiliser is put onto fields? Give full details.

32) What is the big fancy name given to this problem? How can it be avoided?

Atoms

The structure of atoms is simple — there's almost nothing to them. Read, enjoy and learn.

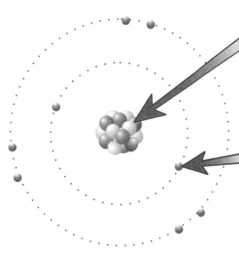

Atoms are <u>really tiny</u>, don't forget. They're <u>too small to see</u> with an ordinary microscope.

The Nucleus

1) It's in the <u>middle</u> of the atom.
2) It contains <u>protons</u> and <u>neutrons</u>.
3) It has a <u>positive charge</u> because of the protons.
4) Almost the <u>whole</u> mass of the atom is <u>concentrated</u> in the nucleus.
5) But size-wise it's <u>tiny</u> compared to the rest of the atom.

The Electrons

1) Move <u>around</u> the nucleus.
2) They're <u>negatively charged</u>.
3) They're <u>tiny</u>, but they cover <u>a lot of space</u>.
4) The <u>volume</u> their orbits occupy determines how big the atom is.
5) They have <u>virtually no mass</u>.
6) They occupy <u>shells</u> around the nucleus.
7) These shells explain <u>the whole of Chemistry</u>.

Number of Protons Equals Number of Electrons

1) Neutral atoms have <u>no charge</u> overall.
2) The <u>charge</u> on the electrons is the <u>same</u> size as the charge on the <u>protons</u> but <u>opposite</u>.
3) This means the <u>number</u> of <u>protons</u> always equals the <u>number</u> of <u>electrons</u> in a <u>neutral atom</u>.
4) If some electrons are <u>added</u> or <u>removed</u>, the atom becomes <u>charged</u> and is then an <u>ion</u>.
5) The number of neutrons isn't fixed but is usually <u>just a bit higher</u> than the number of protons.

Use Atomic Number and Mass Number to Describe an Atom

These two numbers tell you how many of each kind of particle an atom has.

<u>Protons</u> are <u>Heavy</u> and <u>Positively Charged</u>
<u>Neutrons</u> are <u>Heavy</u> and <u>Neutral</u>
<u>Electrons</u> are <u>Tiny</u> and <u>Negatively Charged</u>

PARTICLE	MASS	CHARGE
Proton	1	+1
Neutron	1	0
Electron	$\frac{1}{2000}$	−1

(<u>Electron mass</u> is often taken as <u>zero</u>.)

THE MASS NUMBER → **23**
— Total of Protons and Neutrons

THE ATOMIC NUMBER → **11** **Na**
— Number of Protons

Points to Note

1) The <u>atomic (proton) number</u> tells you how many <u>protons</u> there are.
2) This <u>also</u> tells you how many <u>electrons</u> there are.
3) The <u>atomic number</u> is what distinguishes one particular element from another.
4) To get the number of <u>neutrons</u> — just <u>subtract</u> the <u>atomic number</u> from the <u>mass number</u>.
5) The <u>mass (nucleon) number</u> is always the <u>biggest</u> number. It tells you the relative mass of the atom.
6) The <u>mass number</u> is always roughly <u>double</u> the <u>proton</u> number.
7) Which means there's about the <u>same</u> number of protons as neutrons in any nucleus.

Basic Atom facts — they don't take up much space...

This stuff on atoms should be permanently engraved in the minds of everyone.
I don't understand how people can get through the day without knowing this stuff, really I don't.
<u>Learn it now</u>, and watch as the Universe unfolds and reveals its timeless mysteries to you...

Isotopes, Elements and Compounds

Isotopes are the Same except for an Extra Neutron or two

A favourite trick Exam question: "Explain what is meant by the term Isotope". The trick is that it's impossible to explain what one isotope is. You have to outsmart them and always start your answer "ISOTOPES ARE..."

> ISOTOPES ARE: different atomic forms of the same element, which have the SAME number of PROTONS but a DIFFERENT number of NEUTRONS.

1) The upshot is: isotopes must have the same atomic number but different mass numbers.
2) If they had different atomic numbers, they'd be different elements altogether.
3) A very popular pair of isotopes are carbon-12 and carbon-14.

Carbon-12

$^{12}_{6}C$

6 PROTONS
6 ELECTRONS
6 NEUTRONS

Carbon-14

$^{14}_{6}C$

6 PROTONS
6 ELECTRONS
8 NEUTRONS

The number of electrons decides the chemistry of the element. If the atomic number is the same, then the number of protons is the same, so the number of electrons is the same, so the chemistry is the same. The different number of neutrons in the nucleus doesn't affect the chemical behaviour at all.

Elements consist of One Type of atom only

Elements cannot be broken down chemically. Quite a lot of everyday substances are elements:

 Copper

 Aluminium

 Iron

 Oxygen

 Nitrogen

Mixtures are Easily Separated — Compounds are Chemically Bonded

1) Air is a mixture of gases — the oxygen, nitrogen, argon and carbon dioxide can be easily separated out.
2) There is no chemical bond between the different parts of a mixture.
3) The properties of a mixture are just a mixture of the properties of the separate parts.
4) A mixture of iron powder and sulphur powder will show the properties of both iron and sulphur. It will contain grey magnetic bits of iron and bright yellow bits of sulphur.

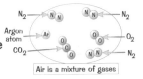
Air is a mixture of gases

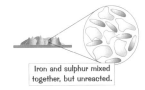
Iron and sulphur mixed together, but unreacted.

①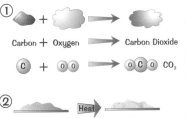

Carbon + Oxygen ⟶ Carbon Dioxide

C + O O ⟶ O C O CO₂

5) Carbon dioxide is a compound formed from a chemical reaction between carbon and oxygen.
6) It's very difficult to separate the two original elements out again.
7) The properties of a compound are totally different from the properties of the original elements.

②

Fe + S ⟶ Fe S FeS
Mixture   Compound

8) If iron and sulphur react to form iron sulphide, the compound formed is a grey solid lump, and doesn't behave anything like either iron or sulphur.

Don't mix these up — it'll only compound your problems...

Elements, mixtures and compounds. To most people they sound like basically the same thing. *Ha!* Not to GCSE Examiners they don't, pal! You make mighty sure you remember their different names and the differences between them. Just more easy marks to be won or lost.

The Periodic Table

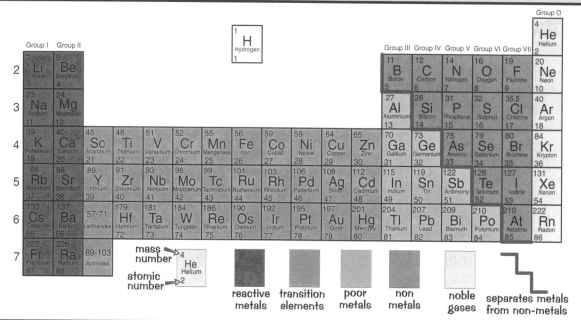

reactive metals | transition elements | poor metals | non metals | noble gases | separates metals from non-metals

The Periodic Table is Ace

1) There are 100ish elements, which all materials are made of. More are still being discovered.
2) The modern Periodic Table shows the elements in order of ascending atomic number.
3) The Periodic Table is laid out so that elements with similar properties form in columns.
4) These vertical columns are called Groups and Roman Numerals are often (but not always) used for them.
5) For example the Group 2 elements are Be, Mg, Ca, Sr, Ba and Ra.
   They're all metals which form 2+ ions and they have many other similar properties.
6) The Group to which the element belongs corresponds to the number of electrons it has in its outer shell.
   Eg. Group 1 elements have 1 outer shell electron, Group 4 elements have 4 outer shell electrons and so on.
7) The rows are called periods. Each new period represents another full shell of electrons.
8) The period to which the element belongs corresponds to the number of shells of electrons it has.
   Eg. sodium in period 3 has 3 shells of electrons.

The Elements of a Group Have the Same Outer Electrons

1) The elements in each Group all have the same number of electrons in their outer shell.
2) That's why they have similar properties. And that's why we arrange them in this way.
3) You absolutely must get that into your head if you want to understand any Chemistry.

   The properties of the elements are decided entirely by how many electrons they have.
   Atomic number is therefore very significant because it is equal to how many electrons each atom has.
   But it's the number of electrons in the outer shell which is the really important thing.

Electron Shells are just Totally Brill

The fact that electrons form shells around atoms is the basis for the whole of Chemistry.
If they just whizzed round the nucleus any old how and didn't care about shells or any of that stuff there'd be no chemical reactions. No nothing in fact — because nothing would happen.
   Without shells there'd be no atoms wanting to gain, lose or share electrons to form full shell arrangements. So they wouldn't be interested in forming ions or covalent bonds. Nothing would bother and nothing would happen. The atoms would just slob about, all day long. Just like teenagers.
   But amazingly, they do form shells (if they didn't, we wouldn't even be here to wonder about it), and the electron arrangement of each atom determines the whole of its chemical behaviour.
Phew. I mean electron arrangements explain practically the whole Universe. They're just totally brill.

Electron Shells — where would we be without them...

Make sure you learn the whole periodic table including every name, symbol and number.
No, only kidding! Just learn the numbered points and scribble them down, mini-essay style.

Electron Shells

The fact that electrons occupy "shells" around the nucleus is what causes the whole of Chemistry. Remember that, and watch how it applies to each bit of it. It's ace.

Electron Shell Rules:

1) Electrons always occupy <u>shells</u> (sometimes called <u>energy levels</u>).
2) The <u>lowest</u> energy levels are <u>always filled first</u>.
3) Only <u>a certain number</u> of electrons are allowed in each shell:
   <u>1st shell</u>: 2   <u>2nd Shell</u>: 8   <u>3rd Shell</u>: 8
4) Atoms are much <u>happier</u> when they have <u>full electron shells</u>.
5) In most atoms the <u>outer shell</u> is <u>not full</u> and this makes the atom want to <u>react</u>.

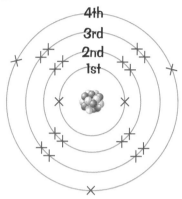

4th shell still filling

Working out Electron Configurations

You need to know the <u>electron configurations</u> for the first <u>20</u> elements. They're shown in the diagram below — but they're not hard to work out. For a quick example, take Nitrogen. <u>Follow the steps</u>...

1) The periodic table tells you that Nitrogen has <u>seven</u> protons... so it must have <u>seven</u> electrons.

2) Follow the 'Electron Shell Rules' above. The <u>first</u> shell can only take 2 electrons and the <u>second</u> shell can take a <u>maximum</u> of 8 electrons.

3) So the electron configuration for Nitrogen must be 2,5 — easy peasy.

4) Now <u>you</u> try it for argon.

The Periodic Table has a big gap here where the transition metals fit in on row four.

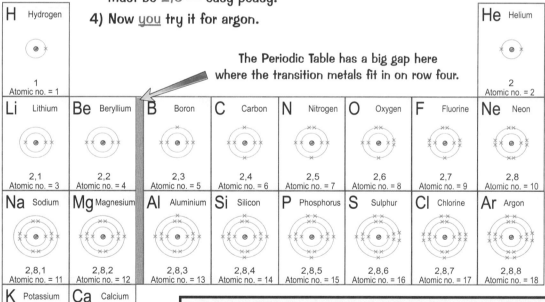

<u>Answer:</u> To calculate the electron configuration of argon, <u>follow the rules</u>. It's got 18 protons, so it <u>must</u> have 18 electrons. The first shell must have <u>2</u> electrons, the second shell must have <u>8</u>, and so the third shell must have <u>8</u> as well. It's as easy as <u>2, 8, 8</u>.

Electron shells rule...

There's some really important stuff on this page and you really do need to <u>learn all of it</u>. Once you have, it'll make all of the rest of the stuff in this book an awful lot easier. So practise calculating <u>electron configurations</u> and drawing <u>electron shell</u> diagrams.

Ionic Bonding

Ionic Bonding — Swapping Electrons

In ionic bonding, atoms lose or gain electrons to form charged particles (or ions) which are then strongly attracted to one another, (because of the attraction of opposite charges, + and –).

A shell with just one electron is well keen to get rid...

All the atoms over at the left hand side of the periodic table, such as sodium, potassium, calcium etc. have just one or two electrons in their outer shell. And basically they're pretty keen to get shot of them, because then they'll only have full shells left, which is how they like it.
So given half a chance they do get rid, and that leaves the atom as an ion instead.
Now ions aren't the kind of things to sit around quietly watching the world go by.
They tend to leap at the first passing ion with an opposite charge and stick to it like glue.

A nearly full shell is well keen to get that extra electron...

On the other side of the Periodic Table, the elements in Group Six and Group Seven, such as oxygen and chlorine have outer shells which are nearly full. They're obviously pretty keen to gain that extra one or two electrons to fill the shell up. When they do of course they become ions — you know, not the kind of things to sit around, and before you know it, pop, they've latched onto the atom (ion) that gave up the electron a moment earlier. The reaction of sodium and chlorine is a classic case:

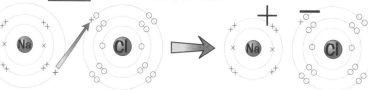

(1) The sodium atom gives up its outer electron and becomes an Na$^+$ ion.

(2) The chlorine atom picks up the spare electron and becomes a Cl$^-$ ion.

(3) POP!
An ionic bond is formed.

Simple Ions — Groups 1 & 2 and 6 & 7

1) Ions are charged particles — they can be single atoms (eg. Cl$^-$) or groups of atoms (eg. NO$_3^-$).

2) When atoms lose or gain electrons to form ions, all they're trying to do is get a full outer shell. Atoms like full outer shells — it's atom heaven.

3) When metals form ions, they lose electrons to form positive ions. Loss of electrons is called oxidation.

4) When non-metals form ions, they gain electrons to form negative ions. Gain of electrons is called reduction.

5) So when a metal and a non-metal combine, they form ionic bonds.

6) You need to know the positive and negative ions in the table on the right.

7) To work out the formula of an ionic compound, you have to balance the +ve and the –ve charges.

POSITIVE (+ve) IONS		NEGATIVE (–ve) IONS	
Group 1	Group 2	Group 6	Group 7
Li$^+$	Be^{2+}	O^{2-}	F$^-$
Na$^+$	Mg^{2+}		Cl$^-$
K$^+$	Ca^{2+}		

Lithium fluoride
Li$^+$ + F$^-$ ⟶ LiF
The lithium ion is 1+, and the fluoride ion is 1–, so they balance.

Potassium oxide
2 K$^+$ + O^{2-} ⟶ K$_2$O
The potassium ion is 1+, and the oxygen ion is 2–, so you need two K$^+$ ions to balance the O^{2-} ion.

Magnesium chloride
Mg^{2+} + 2 Cl$^-$ ⟶ MgCl$_2$
The magnesium ion is 2+, and the chloride ion is 1–, so you need two Cl$^-$ ions to balance the Mg^{2+} ion.

Full Shells — it's the name of the game, pal...

Make sure you know exactly how and why ionic bonds are formed. There are quite a lot of words on this page but only to hammer home two basic points:
1) Ionic bonds involve swapping electrons 2) Some atoms like to lose them, some like to gain them.

Electron Shells and Ions

Electronic Structure of some Simple ions

"Dot and cross" diagrams show what happens to the electrons in an ionic bond:

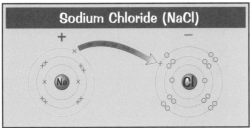

The sodium atom gives up its outer electron, becoming a Na⁺ ion. The chlorine atom picks up the electron, becoming a Cl⁻ (chloride) ion.

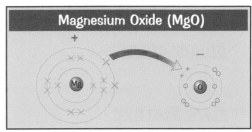

The magnesium atom gives up its two outer electrons, becoming a Mg^{2+} ion. The oxygen atom picks up the electrons, becoming an O^{2-} (oxide) ion.

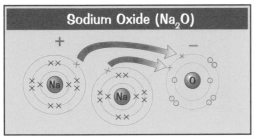

Two sodium atoms give up their outer electrons, becoming two Na⁺ ions. The oxygen atom picks up the two electrons, becoming an O^{2-} ion.

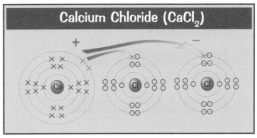

The calcium atom gives up its two outer electrons, becoming a Ca^{2+} ion. The two chlorine atoms pick up one electron each, becoming two Cl⁻ (chloride) ions.

Notice that all the atoms end up with full outer shells as a result of this giving and taking of electrons.

Giant Ionic Structures don't melt easily, but when they do...

1) Ionic bonds always produce giant ionic structures.
2) The ions form a closely packed regular lattice arrangement. The ions are not free to move though, so these compounds do not conduct electricity when solid.
3) There are very strong chemical bonds between all the ions.
4) A single crystal of sodium chloride (salt) is one giant ionic lattice, which is why salt crystals tend to be cuboid in shape.

1) They have High Melting Points and Boiling Points...

...due to the very strong chemical bonds between all the ions in the giant structure.

2) They Dissolve to form solutions that Conduct Electricity

When dissolved the ions separate and are all free to move in the solution, so obviously they'll carry electric current.

3) They Conduct electricity when Molten

When it melts, the ions are free to move and they'll carry electric current.

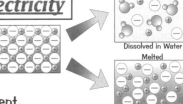

Dissolved in Water / Melted

Simple ions — looks simple enough to me...

Yet again, more stuff you've got to know. LEARN which atoms form 1+, 1–, 2+ and 2– ions, and why. You need to know the structure of giant ionic substances, and their properties too. When you think you've got it, cover the page and start scribbling to see what you really know. Then look back, learn the bits you missed, and try again. And again.

Group 1 — Alkali Metals

They're called 'alkali metals' because their <u>hydroxides</u> dissolve in <u>water</u> to give an <u>alkaline</u> solution. Simple.

Learn These Trends:

As you go <u>DOWN</u> Group I, the Alkali Metals become:

1) *Bigger atoms*

...because there's one extra full shell of electrons for each row you go down.

2) *More Reactive*

...because the outer electron is more easily lost, because it's further from the nucleus.

3) *Higher density*

because the atoms have more mass.

4) *Even Softer to cut* (they're all pretty soft)

5) *Lower melting point*

They have comparatively low melting points.

6) *Lower boiling point*

Group I	Group II
7 Li Lithium 3	Be
23 Na Sodium 11	Mg
39 K Potassium 19	Ca
85.5 Rb Rubidium 37	Sr
133 Cs Caesium 55	Ba
223 Fr Francium 87	Ra

These <u>Group II</u> metals are quite similar to Group I, except that they have two electrons in the outer shell and form 2+ ions. They are less reactive.

1) The Alkali metals are very Reactive

They have to be <u>stored in oil</u> because they react with air and water.
And they need to be handled with forceps because they burn the skin.

2) They are: Lithium, Sodium, Potassium and a couple more

Know those three names real well. They may also mention Rubidium and Caesium.

3) The Alkali metals all have ONE outer electron

This makes them very <u>reactive</u> and gives them all similar properties.

4) The Alkali metals all form 1⁺ ions

They are <u>keen to lose</u> their one outer electron to form a 1^+ ion. The more reactive the alkali metal the happier it is to lose an electron. (Losing electrons is known as <u>oxidation</u>.)

5) The Alkali metals always form Ionic Compounds

They are so keen to lose the outer electron there's <u>no way</u> they'd consider <u>sharing</u>, so covalent bonding is <u>out of the question</u>.

6) The Alkali metals are soft — they cut with a knife

Lithium is the hardest, but still easy to cut with a scalpel.
They're <u>shiny</u> when freshly cut, but <u>soon go dull</u> as they react with the air.

7) The Alkali metals melt and boil easily (for metals)

Lithium melts at 180°C, Caesium at 29°C. Lithium boils at 1330°C, Caesium at 670°C.

8) The Alkali metals have low density (they float)

Lithium, Sodium and Potassium are all <u>less dense than water</u>.
The others "<u>float</u>" anyway, on the H_2 bubbles (see next page).

Learn about Alkali Metals — or get your fingers burnt...

Now we're getting into the seriously dreary facts section. This takes a bit of learning. <u>Enjoy</u>.

Reactions of the Alkali Metals

Reaction with Cold Water produces Hydrogen Gas

1) When lithium, sodium or potassium are put in water, they react very vigorously.

2) They move around the surface, fizzing furiously.

3) They produce hydrogen. Potassium gets hot enough to ignite it. A lighted splint will indicate hydrogen by producing the notorious "squeaky pop" as the H_2 ignites.

4) Sodium and potassium melt in the heat of the reaction.

5) They form a hydroxide in solution, ie. aqueous OH^- ions.

$$2Na_{(s)} + 2H_2O_{(l)} \rightarrow 2NaOH_{(aq)} + H_{2(g)}$$

$$2K_{(s)} + 2H_2O_{(l)} \rightarrow 2KOH_{(aq)} + H_{2(g)}$$

The solution becomes alkaline, which changes the colour of the pH indicator to purple.

Alkali Metals Burn in Air to produce Oxides

They all burn in air with pretty coloured flames:

Lithium: $4Li_{(s)} + O_{2(g)} \rightarrow 2Li_2O_{(s)}$ (lithium oxide)   Bright red flame

Sodium: $4Na_{(s)} + O_{2(g)} \rightarrow 2Na_2O_{(s)}$ (sodium oxide)   Bright orange flame

Potassium: $4K_{(s)} + O_{2(g)} \rightarrow 2K_2O_{(s)}$ (potassium oxide)   Bright lilac flame

Use a Flame Test to Identify Which Metal is Present

1) You can use a flame test to identify the positive ion (ie. the metal ion) in a compound. Flame tests make use of the fact that many metals (and their compounds) burn with a distinctive colour flame.

2) If you know that a compound contains an alkali metal, but you're not sure which one — you just burn a small amount of the substance.

3) The colour of the flame tells you which alkali metal is present.

Lilac flame so contains potassium.

Alkali Metal Oxides and Hydroxides are Alkaline

This means that they'll react with acids to form neutral salts, like this:

$$NaOH + HCl \rightarrow H_2O + NaCl \text{ (salt)}$$

$$Na_2O + 2HCl \rightarrow H_2O + 2NaCl \text{ (salt)}$$

All Alkali Compounds look like 'Salt' and Dissolve with Glee

1) All alkali metal compounds are ionic, so they form crystals which dissolve easily.

2) They're all very stable because the alkali metals are so reactive.

3) Because they always form ionic compounds with giant ionic lattices the compounds all look pretty much like the regular 'salt' you put in your chip butties.

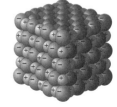

The Notorious Squeaky Pop? — weren't they a Rock Band...

This stuff's pretty grisly isn't it. Still, if you keep covering the page and repeating bits back to yourself, or scribbling bits down, then little by little it does go in. Little by little. Nicely.

Group 7 — The Halogens

Learn These Trends:

As you go **DOWN** Group VII, the **HALOGENS** have the following properties:

1) <u>Less Reactive</u> because there's less inclination to gain the extra electron to fill the outer shell when it's further out from the nucleus.
2) <u>Higher melting point</u>
3) <u>Higher boiling point</u>

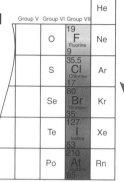

Halogens — Non-Metals with Coloured Vapours

<u>Chlorine</u> is a fairly reactive, poisonous, <u>dense green gas</u>.
<u>Bromine</u> is a dense, poisonous, <u>orange liquid</u>.
<u>Iodine</u> is a <u>dark grey crystalline solid</u>.

They all form molecules which are pairs of atoms

F_2 Cl_2 Br_2  I_2

The Halogens do Both Ionic and Covalent Bonding

The Halogens all form <u>ions with a 1⁻ charge</u>: F^- Cl^- Br^- I^- as in Na^+Cl^- or $Fe^{3+}Br_3^-$
They form <u>covalent bonds</u> with <u>themselves</u> and in various <u>molecular compounds</u> like these:

<u>Carbon tetrachloride:</u>
(CCl_4)

<u>Hydrogen chloride:</u>
(HCl)

The Halogens react with Alkali Metals to form Salts

They react vigorously with alkali metals to form <u>salts</u> (or '<u>metal halides</u>').

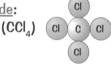

$$2Na_{(s)} + Cl_{2(g)} \rightarrow 2NaCl_{(s)}$$
(Sodium chloride)

$$2K_{(s)} + Br_{2(g)} \rightarrow 2KBr_{(s)}$$
(Potassium bromide)

More reactive Halogens will displace less reactive ones

Cl_2 gas

<u>Chlorine</u> can displace <u>bromine</u> and <u>iodine</u> from a solution of <u>bromide</u> or <u>iodide</u>.
<u>Bromine</u> will also displace <u>iodine</u> because of the <u>trend</u> in <u>reactivity</u>.

Solution of Potassium iodide
Iodine forming in solution

$$Cl_{2(g)} + 2KI_{(aq)} \rightarrow I_{2(aq)} + 2KCl_{(aq)}$$
$$Cl_{2(g)} + 2KBr_{(aq)} \rightarrow Br_{2(aq)} + 2KCl_{(aq)}$$

Uses of Halogens

1) <u>Chlorine compounds</u> are used to <u>sterilise</u> swimming pools and drinking water.
2) <u>Chlorine</u> is used to make <u>pesticides</u>, and in the manufacture of the plastic <u>PVC</u> (<u>polyvinyl chloride</u>).
3) <u>Iodine</u> is used to <u>sterilise wounds</u>, but it stings like nobody's business and stains the skin brown.

I've never liked Halogens — they give me a bad head...

Well, I think Halogens are just slightly less grim than the Alkali metals. At least they change colour and go from gases to liquid to solid. <u>Learn the boring facts anyway</u>. And smile ☺.

Group 8 — The Noble Gases

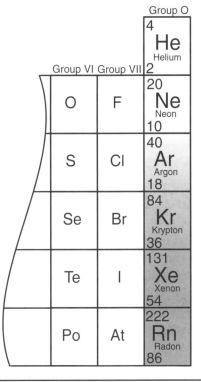

As you go down the Group:

1) The density increases
because the atomic mass increases.

2) The boiling point increases
Helium boils at –269°C (that's cold!)
Xenon boils at –108°C (that's still cold)

They all have full outer shells
— that's why they're so inert

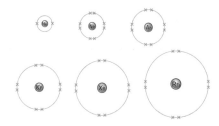

It's actually the arrangement of the 8 outermost electrons in a noble gas that makes them unreactive — so this arrangement of electrons is called a stable octet.

HELIUM, NEON, ARGON AND KRYPTON ARE NOBLE GASES

There's also Xenon and Radon, which you may get asked about.
They're sometimes called the Inert gases. 'Inert' means "doesn't react".

THEY'RE ALL COLOURLESS, MONATOMIC GASES

Most gases are made up of molecules, but noble gases only exist as individual atoms, because they won't form bonds with anything.

THE NOBLE GASES DON'T REACT AT ALL

Helium, Neon and Argon don't form any kind of chemical bonds with anything.
They always exist as separate atoms. They won't even join up in pairs.

HELIUM IS USED IN AIRSHIPS AND PARTY BALLOONS

Helium is ideal: it has very low density (lower than air so it floats)
and won't set on fire, (like hydrogen does!).

NEON AND KRYPTON ARE USED IN ELECTRICAL DISCHARGE TUBES

Neon and Krypton are used in fluorescent lighting.

ARGON IS USED IN FILAMENT LAMPS (LIGHT BULBS)

It provides an inert atmosphere which stops the very hot
filament from burning away.

HELIUM, NEON AND ARGON ARE USED IN LASERS TOO

There's the famous little red Helium-Neon laser
and the more powerful Argon laser.

They don't react — that's Noble De-use to us Chemists...

Well they don't react so there's obviously not much to learn about these. Nevertheless, there's likely to be several questions on them so make sure you learn everything on this page.

Transition Metals

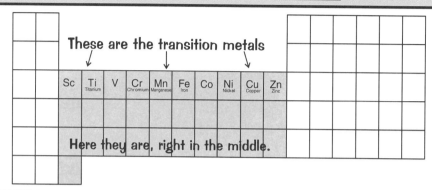

These are the transition metals

| Sc | Ti Titanium | V | Cr Chromium | Mn Manganese | Fe Iron | Co | Ni Nickel | Cu Copper | Zn Zinc |

Here they are, right in the middle.

1) They are Chromium, Manganese, Iron, Nickel, Copper, Zinc...

A lot of everyday metals are transition metals (eg. copper, chromium, zinc, gold, silver, platinum) — but there are loads of others as well. If you get asked about a transition metal you've never heard of — don't panic. These "new" transition metals follow all the properties you've already learnt for the others. It's just that some folk get worried by the unfamiliar names.

2) They all have high melting and boiling points, and high density

They're typical metals. They have the properties you would expect of a proper metal:

1) Good conductors of heat and electricity.
2) Very dense, strong and lustrous (ie. shiny).
3) Iron melts at 1500°C and boils at 2750°C. Copper melts at 1100°C and boils at 2567°C.

3) Transition Metals and their Compounds make Good Catalysts

1) Iron is the catalyst used in the Haber process for making ammonia.
2) Nickel is useful for the hydrogenation of alkenes.

4) The Compounds are very Colourful

The compounds are colourful due to the transition metal ion they contain.
  eg. Iron (II) compounds are usually light green.
       Iron (III) compounds are usually orange/brown (eg. rust).
       Copper compounds are often blue.

5) Iron is made into Steel which is Cheap and Strong

Iron and steel:
  ADVANTAGES: Cheap and strong.
  DISADVANTAGES: Heavy, prone to rusting.

  Steel may rust and it may not be exactly "space age" but it's strong and it's awful cheap, and it still has a lot of uses.

Iron and steel are used for:
1) Construction such as bridges and buildings.
2) Cars and lorries and trains and boats and NOT PLANES and push-bikes and tanks and pianos...
3) Stainless steel doesn't rust and is used for pans and for fixtures on boats.

6) Copper: Good Conductor, Easily Bent and Doesn't Corrode

This is a winning combination which makes it ideal for:

1) Water pipes and gas pipes, because it can be bent to shape by hand without fracturing.
2) Electrical wiring because it can be easily bent round corners and it conducts really well.
3) Forms useful non corroding alloys such as brass (for trumpets) and bronze (for statues).
  DRAWBACKS: Copper is quite expensive and is not strong.

Lots of pretty colours — that's what we like to see...

There's quite a few things to learn about transition metals. First try to remember the six headings. Then learn the details that go under each one. Keep trying to scribble it all down.

Thermal Decomposition and Precipitation

1) Thermal Decomposition — Breaking Down with Heat

1) Thermal decomposition is when a substance breaks down into simpler substances when heated.
2) It's different from a reaction because there's only one substance to start with.
3) Transition metal carbonates break down on heating. Transition metal carbonates are things like copper carbonate ($CuCO_3$), iron (II) carbonate ($FeCO_3$), zinc carbonate ($ZnCO_3$) and manganese carbonate ($MnCO_3$), ie. they've all got a CO_3 bit in them.
4) They break down into a metal oxide (eg. copper oxide, CuO) and carbon dioxide. This usually results in a colour change in the substance.

EXAMPLE: The thermal decomposition of copper carbonate.

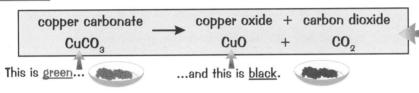

copper carbonate $\longrightarrow$ copper oxide + carbon dioxide
$CuCO_3$ $\qquad$ CuO + CO_2

This is green... ...and this is black.

The reactions for the thermal decomposition of:
(i) iron (II) carbonate,
(ii) manganese carbonate,
(iii) zinc carbonate,
are the same — although the colours are different.

Use Limewater to test for Carbon Dioxide

1) You can easily check that the gas given off is carbon dioxide.
2) Bubble the gas through limewater — if it is carbon dioxide, the limewater turns milky.

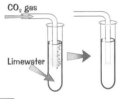

CO_2 gas

Limewater

2) Precipitation — A Solid Forms in Solution

1) A precipitation reaction is where two solutions react and a solid forms in the solution and sinks.
2) The solid is said to 'precipitate out' and, confusingly, the solid is also called 'a precipitate'.
3) Some soluble transition metal salts react with sodium hydroxide to form an insoluble hydroxide, which then precipitates out.

EXAMPLE: Soluble copper sulphate reacts with sodium hydroxide to form insoluble copper hydroxide.

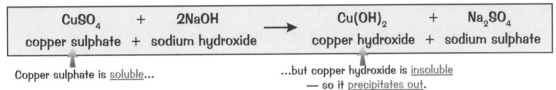

$CuSO_4$ $\quad$ + $\quad$ $2NaOH$ $\qquad \longrightarrow \qquad$ $Cu(OH)_2$ $\quad$ + $\quad$ Na_2SO_4
copper sulphate + sodium hydroxide $\qquad\qquad$ copper hydroxide + sodium sulphate

Copper sulphate is soluble...

...but copper hydroxide is insoluble — so it precipitates out.

4) Since copper hydroxide is blue, you get a distinctive blue precipitate forming in the test tube.
5) You can also write the above equation in terms of ions:

$$Cu^{2+} \ + \ 2OH^- \longrightarrow Cu(OH)_2$$

The Cu^{2+} ions and the hydroxide ions combine to give you the insoluble copper hydroxide.

Use Precipitation to test for Transition Metal Ions

1) Some insoluble transition metal hydroxides are distinctive colours.
2) You can use this fact to test which transition metal ions a solution contains.
3) If you add sodium hydroxide to an unknown soluble salt, and an orange precipitate forms, you know you had iron(III) ions in the solution.

Copper hydroxide is a blue solid.
Iron (II) hydroxide is a grey/green solid.
Iron (III) hydroxide is an orangey solid.

My duffel coat's worn out — thermal decomposition...

Thermal decomposition might sound fun, but it isn't. Trouble is, you still need to know about it, especially the equations. Precipitation is a bit better — but there's still loads of equations to get your head around, and you need to know the colours of those precipitates. Learn it all.

Revision Summary for Module CD6

These certainly aren't the easiest questions you're going to come across. That's because they test what you know without giving you any clues. At first you might think they're impossibly difficult. Eventually you'll realise that they simply test whether you've learnt the stuff or not.
If you're struggling to answer these then you need to do some serious learning.

1) What are the three particles found in an atom? What are their relative masses and charges?

2) What do the mass number and atomic number represent?

3) Explain what an isotope is. Give a well-known example.

4) What's the difference between elements, mixtures and compounds?

5) What feature of atoms determines the order of the modern Periodic Table?

6) What are the Periods and Groups? Explain their significance in terms of electrons.

7) List five facts (or "Rules") about electron shells.

8) Calculate the electron configuration for each of the following elements: $^{4}_{2}He$, $^{12}_{6}C$, $^{31}_{15}P$, $^{39}_{19}K$.

9) Draw diagrams to show the electron arrangements for the first twenty elements.

10) What is ionic bonding? Which kind of atoms like to do ionic bonding? Why is this?

11) Which atoms form 1+, 1−, 2+ and 2− ions?

12) Sketch the dot and cross diagrams for: a) Sodium Chloride
                                               b) Magnesium Oxide
                                               c) Sodium Oxide
                                               d) Calcium Chloride

13) Draw a diagram of a giant ionic lattice and give three features of giant ionic structures.

14) What are the electron arrangements of the noble gases? What are their properties?

15) Why are the noble gases so unreactive?

16) Name four inert gases and give uses for them.

17) Which Group are the alkali metals? What is their outer shell like?

18) Give details of the reactions of the alkali metals with water.

19) List four physical properties, and two chemical properties of the alkali metals.

20) Describe the trends in appearance and reactivity of the halogens as you go down the Group.

21) List four properties common to all the halogens. Write down four uses of halogens.

22) Give details, with equations, of the reaction of the halogens with alkali metals.

23) Give details, with equations, of a displacement reaction involving the halogens.

24) List four properties of transition metals, and two properties of their compounds.

25) Name six transition metals, and give uses for two of them.

26) What are thermal decomposition reactions?

27) What type of reaction between two liquids results in the formation of a solid?
    What are these solid products called?

28) Describe a way to test solutions for transition metal ions.

Current, Voltage and Resistance

Isn't electricity great. Mind you, it's pretty bad news if the words don't mean anything to you — so don't even think about skipping this bit...

1) *CURRENT (I)* is the flow of electrons round the circuit.
2) *VOLTAGE (V)* is the driving force that pushes the current round. Kind of like "electrical pressure".
3) *RESISTANCE (R)* is anything in the circuit which slows the flow down.
4) THERE'S A *BALANCE*: the voltage is trying to push the current round the circuit, and the resistance is opposing it — the relative sizes of the voltage and resistance decide how big the current will be:

> If you increase the *VOLTAGE* — then *MORE CURRENT* will flow.
> If you increase the *RESISTANCE* — then *LESS CURRENT* will flow.

It's Just Like the Flow of Water Around a Set of Pipes

1) A complete loop is needed for a circuit — this lets the current move around like the flow of water.
2) Voltage is like the pressure provided by a pump which pushes the stuff round.
3) Resistance is any sort of constriction in the flow, which is what the pressure has to work against.
4) If you turn up the pump and provide more pressure (or "voltage"), the flow will increase.
5) If you put in more constrictions ("resistance"), the flow (current) will decrease.

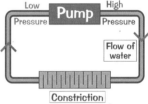

In Metals the Current is Carried by Electrons

1) Electric current will only flow if there are charges which can move freely.
2) Metals contain a "sea" of free electrons (which are negatively charged) and which flow throughout the metal.
3) This is what allows electric current to flow so well in all metals.

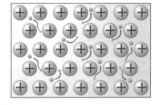

But Electrons Flow the Opposite Way to Conventional Current

We normally say that current in a circuit flows from positive to negative. Alas, electrons were discovered long after that was decided and they turned out to be negatively charged — unlucky. This means they actually flow from –ve to +ve, opposite to the flow of "conventional current".

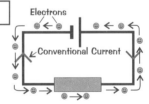

In Electrolytes, Current is Carried by Both +ve and –ve Charges

1) Electrolytes are liquids which contain charges that can move freely.
2) They are either ions dissolved in water, like salt solution, or molten ionic liquids, like molten sodium chloride.
3) When a voltage is applied the positive charges move towards the –ve, and the negative charges move towards the +ve. This is an electric current.

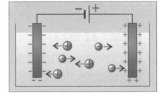

AC Changes Direction but DC Doesn't

Direct current keeps flowing in the same direction all the time — the CRO trace is a horizontal line. DC is supplied by batteries.
Alternating current keeps reversing its direction back and forth — its CRO trace is always a wave. AC is supplied by the mains.
You need to learn these CRO traces — I've not put them in cos they're pretty.

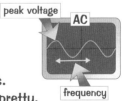

Understanding currents — easy as pie...

This page is all about electric current — what it is, what makes it move, and what tries to stop it. This is the most basic stuff on electricity there is. You realise that you'll never be able to learn anything else about electricity until you know this stuff — don't you? Just checking.

The Standard Test Circuit

This is without doubt the most totally bog-standard circuit the world has ever known. So know it.

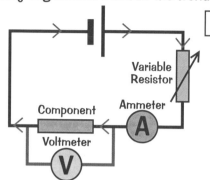

The Ammeter

1) Measures the <u>current</u> in <u>Amperes</u> (<u>Amps</u>) flowing through the component.
2) Must be placed <u>in series</u>.
3) Can be put <u>anywhere</u> in series in the <u>main circuit</u>, but <u>never in parallel</u> like the voltmeter.

The Voltmeter

1) Measures the <u>voltage</u> (in <u>Volts</u>) across the component.
2) Must be placed <u>in parallel</u> around the <u>component under test</u> — <u>NOT</u> around the variable resistor or the battery!
3) The <u>proper</u> name for '<u>voltage</u>' is '<u>potential difference</u>' or '<u>p.d.</u>'.

Five Important Points

1) This <u>very basic circuit</u> is used for <u>testing components</u>, and for getting <u>V-I graphs</u> for them.
2) The <u>component</u>, the <u>ammeter</u> and the <u>variable resistor</u> are all <u>in series</u>, which means they can be put <u>in any order</u> in the main circuit. The <u>voltmeter</u>, on the other hand, can only be placed <u>in parallel</u> around the <u>component under test</u>, as shown. Anywhere else is a definite <u>no-no</u>.
3) As you <u>vary</u> the <u>variable resistor</u> it alters the <u>current</u> flowing through the circuit.
4) This allows you to take several <u>pairs of readings</u> from the <u>ammeter</u> and <u>voltmeter</u>.
5) You can then <u>plot</u> these values for <u>current</u> and <u>voltage</u> on a <u>V-I graph</u>, like the ones below.

Four Hideously Important Voltage-Current (V-I) Graphs

V-I graphs show how the current varies as you change the voltage. Learn these four real well:

Resistor
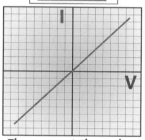

The current through a <u>resistor</u> (at constant temperature) is <u>proportional to voltage</u>.

Different Wires
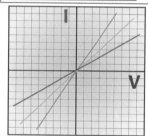

<u>Different wires</u> have different <u>resistances</u>, hence the different <u>slopes</u>.

Filament Lamp
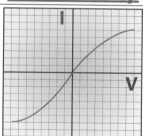

As the <u>temperature</u> of the filament <u>increases</u>, the <u>resistance increases</u>, hence the <u>curve</u>.

Diode
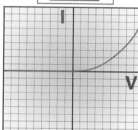

Current will only flow through a diode <u>in one direction</u>, as shown.

Calculating Resistance: R = V/I, (or R = '1/gradient')

For the <u>straight-line graphs</u> the resistance of the component is <u>steady</u> and is equal to the <u>inverse</u> of the <u>gradient</u> of the line, or "<u>1/gradient</u>". In other words, the <u>STEEPER</u> the graph the <u>LOWER</u> the resistance. If the graph <u>curves</u>, it means the resistance is <u>changing</u>. In that case R can be found for any point by taking the <u>pair of values</u> (V,I) from the graph and sticking them in the formula <u>R = V/I</u>. Easy.

All Resistors produce Heat when a Current flows through them

1) This is important. Whenever a <u>current</u> flows through anything with <u>electrical resistance</u> (which is pretty well <u>everything</u>) then <u>electrical energy</u> is converted into <u>heat energy</u>.
2) The <u>more current</u> that flows, the <u>more heat</u> is produced.

In the end, you'll have to learn this — resistance is futile...

There are quite a lot of important details on this page and you need to <u>learn all of them</u>. The only way to make sure you really know it is to <u>cover up the page</u> and see how much of it you can <u>scribble down</u> from <u>memory</u>. Sure, it's not that easy — but it's the only way. Enjoy.

Circuit Symbols and Devices

You have to know all these circuit symbols for the Exam.

Circuit Symbols You Should Know:

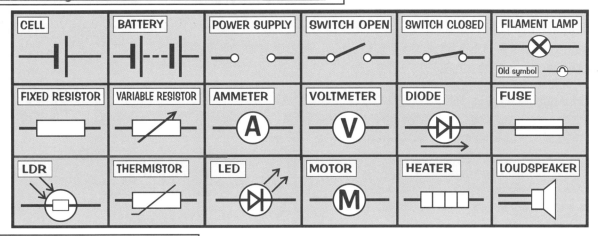

1) Variable Resistor

1) A resistor whose resistance can be changed by twiddling a knob or something.
2) The old-fashioned ones are huge coils of wire with a slider on them.
3) They're great for altering the current flowing through a circuit.
   Turn the resistance up, the current drops. Turn the resistance down, the current goes up.

2) "Semiconductor Diode" or just "Diode"

A special device made from semiconductor material such as silicon. It lets current
flow freely through it in one direction, but not in the other (ie. there's a very high resistance
in the reverse direction). This turns out to be real useful in various electronic circuits.

3) Light Emitting Diode or "LED" to you

1) A diode which gives out light. It only lets current go through in one direction.
2) When it does pass current, it gives out a pretty red or green or yellow light.
3) Stereos usually have lots of jolly little LEDs which light up as the music's playing.

4) Light Dependent Resistor or "LDR" to you

1) In bright light, the resistance falls.
2) In darkness, the resistance is highest.
3) This makes it a useful device for various electronic
   circuits — eg. automatic night lights and burglar detectors.

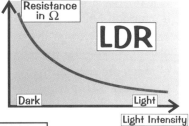

5) Thermistor (Temperature-dependent Resistor)

1) In hot conditions, the resistance drops.
2) In cool conditions, the resistance goes up.
3) Thermistors make useful temperature detectors
   eg. car engine temperature sensors and
   electronic thermostats for central heating.

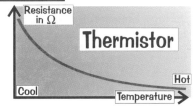

"Diode" — wasn't that a film starring Bruce Willis...

Another page of basic but important details about electrical circuits. You need to know all
those circuit symbols as well as the extra details for the five special devices. When you think
you know it all cover the page and scribble it all down. See how you did, and then try again.

Higher   *Higher*   *Higher*   *Higher*

Static Electricity

Static electricity is all about charges which are not free to move. This causes them to build up in one place and it often ends with a spark or a shock when they do finally move.

1) Build up of Static is Caused by Friction

1) When two insulating materials are rubbed together, electrons will be scraped off one and dumped on the other.

2) This'll leave a positive static charge on one and a negative static charge on the other.

3) Which way the electrons are transferred depends on the two materials involved.

4) Electrically charged objects attract small objects placed near them.
(Try this: rub a comb on a woolly pulley, then put it near tiddly bits of paper and watch them jump.)

5) The classic examples are polythene and acetate rods being rubbed with a cloth duster, as shown in the diagrams:

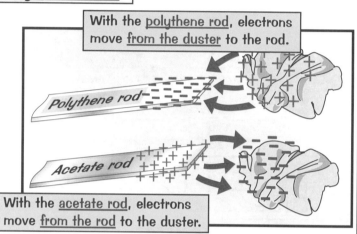

With the polythene rod, electrons move from the duster to the rod.

With the acetate rod, electrons move from the rod to the duster.

2) Only Electrons Move — Never the Positive Charges

Watch out for this in Exams. Both +ve and −ve electrostatic charges are only ever produced by the movement of electrons. The positive charges definitely do not move! A positive static charge is always caused by electrons moving away elsewhere, as shown above. Don't forget!

3) Like Charges Repel, Opposite Charges Attract

This is easy and, I'd have thought, kind of obvious.
Two things with opposite electric charges are attracted to each other.
Two things with the same electric charge will repel each other.
These forces get weaker the further apart the two things are — pretty obviously.

4) Charging by Induction is a bit Tricky

When something which is charged comes near something which isn't, it tends to induce charge, because electrons in the uncharged object move towards or away from the charged object. The result is always the same — the new arrangement of charge always makes the two objects pull together because the repelling charges are now further apart than the attracting charges.
It's tricky, but you can understand it — and you can learn it.

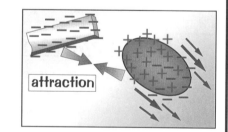
attraction

5) As Charge Builds Up, So Does the Voltage — Causing Sparks

The greater the charge on an isolated object, the greater the voltage between it and the Earth. If the voltage gets big enough there's a spark which jumps across the gap. High voltage cables can be dangerous for this reason. Big sparks have been known to leap from overhead cables to Earth. But not often.

'ZAP!'

A charged conductor can be discharged safely by connecting it to earth with a metal strap.

Phew — it's enough to make your hair stand on end...

The way to tackle this page is to first learn the five headings till you can scribble them all down. Then learn the details for each one, and keep practising by covering the page and scribbling down each heading with as many details as you can remember for each one. Just keep trying...

Static Electricity — Examples

They like asking you to give quite detailed examples in Exams. Make sure you learn all these:

Static Electricity Being Helpful

1) Inkjet Printer:

1) Tiny droplets of ink are forced out of a fine nozzle, making them electrically charged.
2) The droplets are deflected as they pass between two metal plates. A voltage is applied to the plates — one is negative and the other is positive.
3) The droplets are attracted to the plate of the opposite charge and repelled from the plate with the same charge.
4) The size and direction of the voltage across each plate changes so each droplet is deflected to hit a different place on the paper.
5) Loads of tiny dots make up your printout. Clever.

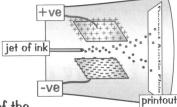

2) Photocopier:

1) The metal plate is electrically charged. An image of what you're copying is projected onto it.
2) Whiter bits of the thing you're copying make light fall on the plate and the charge leaks away.
3) The charged bits attract black powder, which is transferred onto paper.
4) The paper is heated so the powder sticks.
5) Voilà, a photocopy of your piece of paper (or whatever else you've shoved in there).

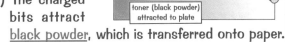

3) Spray Painting and Dust Removal in Chimneys...

These are other uses but photocopiers and inkjet printers are what they really want you to learn.

Static Electricity Being a Little Joker

1) Car Shocks

Air rushing past your car can give it a +ve charge. When you get out and touch the door it gives you a real buzz — in the Exam make sure you say "electrons flow from earth, through you, to neutralise the +ve charge on the car". Some cars have conducting rubber strips which hang down behind the car. This gives a safe discharge to Earth, but spoils all the fun.

2) Clothing Crackles

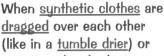

When synthetic clothes are dragged over each other (like in a tumble drier) or over your head, electrons get scraped off. This leaves static charges on both parts, and that leads to the inevitable — attraction (they stick together) and little sparks / shocks as the charges rearrange themselves.

3) Water Pipes

You can also get a shock if you touch a metal water pipe after walking on carpet — walking picks up charge off the carpet, which then flows to Earth down the metal pipe.

Static Electricity Playing at Terrorist

1) Lightning

Rain droplets fall to Earth with positive charge. This creates a huge voltage and a big spark.

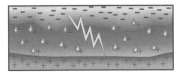

2) Grain Chutes, Paper Rollers and The Fuel Filling Nightmare

1) As fuel flows out of a filler pipe, or paper drags over rollers, or grain shoots out of pipes, then static can build up.
2) This can easily lead to a spark and in dusty or fumy places — BOOM!
3) The solution: make the nozzles or rollers or chutes out of metal so that the charge is conducted away, instead of building up.

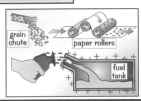

Static electricity — learn the shocking truth...

You really need to learn those two big examples at the top. Your exam board mentions photocopiers and inkjet printers so I bet there'll be a question on them. Crumbs, it's almost relevant to real-life too. Learn the numbered points and keep scribbling them down to check.

Energy Change

There are loads of formulae on this topic, but you've got to know them for the Exam... even if you're not 100% sure what a formula means, learn it, as you'll probably get marks just for being able to write it down.

Calculating Electrical Power

1) The standard formula for <u>electrical power</u> is $P = I \times V$.

2) <u>Power</u> is measured in <u>Watts</u>, <u>Voltage</u> in <u>Volts</u>, and <u>Current</u> in <u>Amps</u>.

3) Most electrical goods indicate their <u>power rating</u> and <u>voltage rating</u>.

   To work out the <u>current</u> that will normally flow use $P = I \times V$, or rather, $I = P/V$.

   <u>EXAMPLE:</u> A hairdrier is rated at 240V, 1.1kW. Find the current which flows.
   <u>ANSWER:</u> I = P/V = 1100/240 = <u>**4.6A**</u>.

Current, Charge, Voltage and Energy Change

Higher

1) Current is the <u>rate of flow of electrical charge</u> around a circuit.
   When <u>current</u> (I) flows past a point in a circuit for a length of <u>time</u> (t)
   then <u>charge</u> (Q) has passed. This is given by the formula: $Q = It$
   More <u>charge</u> passes around the circuit when a <u>bigger current</u> flows.

   <u>EXAMPLE:</u> A car battery supplies a steady current of 12A for sixty seconds.
              How much charge passes during the minute?
   <u>ANSWER:</u> <u>Time</u> (60s), <u>current</u> (12A) and <u>charge</u> are all mentioned in the question.
              The formula with these three in is Q=It, so Q = 12 × 60 = <u>720 C (Coulombs)</u>

2) When electrical <u>charge</u> (Q) goes through a <u>change</u> in voltage (V),
   then <u>energy</u> (E) is <u>transferred</u>.
   Energy is <u>supplied</u> to the charge at the <u>power source</u> to raise it
   through a voltage.
   The charge <u>gives up</u> this energy when it <u>falls</u> through any <u>voltage drop</u> in <u>components</u> elsewhere in the circuit.
   The formula is real simple: $E = QV$

3) The <u>bigger</u> the <u>change</u> in voltage (or p.d.), the <u>more energy</u> (measured in <u>joules</u>) is transferred for a <u>given amount of charge</u> (measured in <u>coulombs</u>) passing through the circuit. That means that a battery with a <u>bigger voltage</u> will supply <u>more energy</u> to the circuit for every <u>coulomb</u> of charge which flows round it, because the charge is raised up '<u>higher</u>' at the start (see diagram) — and as the diagram shows, <u>more energy</u> will be <u>dissipated</u> in the circuit too. This gives rise to <u>two definitions</u> which I guess you should learn, although they're seriously dull:

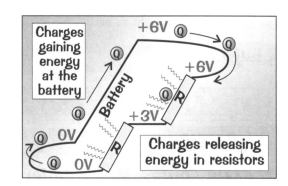

1) <u>**ONE VOLT**</u> is <u>**ONE JOULE PER COULOMB**</u>
2) <u>**VOLTAGE**</u> is the <u>**ENERGY TRANSFERRED PER UNIT CHARGE**</u> passed

Electricity — why does it all turn out so dreary...

I try to make it <u>interesting</u>, really I do. I mean, underneath it all, electricity is pretty good stuff, but somehow every page just seems to end up stuffed full of interminably dreary facts. Well look, I tried, OK. It may be dreary but you've just gotta <u>learn it all</u>, and that's that.

Using Formulae

Always the Same Old Routine

The thing about formulae in Physics is that it's <u>always the same old routine</u>. Once you've learnt how to do it for <u>one</u> formula, you can do it for <u>any other</u>. And that makes the whole thing <u>really simple</u> — but there's still a lot of people who seem to make a real meal of it. Let's take it nice and slowly...

Formula Triangles are Pretty Useful for Getting it Right

<u>All</u> the formulae on the last page can be put into <u>formula triangles</u>.
It's <u>pretty important</u> to learn how to put any formula into a triangle. There are <u>two easy rules</u>:

> 1) If the formula is "<u>A = B×C</u>" then <u>A goes on the top</u> and <u>B×C goes on the bottom</u>.
> 2) If the formula is "<u>A = B/C</u>" then <u>B must go on the top</u> (because that's the only way it'll give "B divided by something") — and so pretty obviously <u>A and C must go on the bottom</u>.

Three Examples:

$V = I \times R$
turns into:

$P = I^2 \times R$
turns into:

$V = E/Q$
turns into:

<u>How to use them:</u> Cover up the thing you want to find and write down what's left showing.
<u>EXAMPLE:</u> To find Q from the last one, cover up Q and you get E/V left showing, so "Q = E/V"

Using Formulae — The Three Rules

> 1) <u>Find a formula</u> which contains <u>the thing you want to find</u>, together with the <u>other things</u> which you've got <u>values</u> for. Convert that formula into a formula triangle.
> 2) <u>Stick</u> the numbers in and <u>work out</u> the answer.
> 3) <u>Think very carefully</u> about all the <u>units</u> — and check that the answer is <u>sensible</u>.

<u>EXAMPLE:</u> A hairdrier is rated at 700W and draws a current of 3A. Find its resistance.
<u>ANSWER:</u> The three quantities mentioned are <u>power</u> (700W), <u>current</u> (3A) and <u>resistance</u>.
  1) The formula with these three in is $P = I^2R$, and the formula triangle version gives us $R = P/I^2$.
  2) Sticking the numbers in: $R = 700/3^2 = 700/9 = 77.78 = \underline{78\Omega}$.
  3) The power and current are already in their proper units of Watts and Amps, so that's OK.
     The answer for R must be given in its proper units too, namely Ω, which we've done.
     The value of 78Ω is fine. If it was $1,000,000\Omega$ or 0.00034Ω you'd worry and check it.

Watch out for the Units

Once you've got the hang of formula triangles there's only one thing left to get wrong — <u>units</u>.
There's <u>two things</u> about units that you have to really watch out for:

> 1) Make sure that the numbers <u>you put into</u> the formula are in <u>standard (SI) units</u>.
> 2) When you write the answer down, make sure your <u>answer</u> has its <u>proper units</u>.

<u>IMPORTANT EXAMPLES:</u> 500g must be turned into 0.5kg, 2 minutes into 120 seconds, 700kJ into 700,000J, 145cm into 1.45m, etc. before putting them into a formula. If you don't put SI units <u>in</u> then the answer won't come <u>out</u> with SI units, which can get tricky unless you know what you're doing.

Formulae — aren't they just fabulous...

Physics formulae are <u>amazingly repetitive</u>. You really must get it into your head that they're basically <u>all the same</u>. This page has the <u>simple rules</u> that would allow <u>anyone</u> to work out the answers without really knowing anything about Physics at all. It's easy peasy, surely it is.

Revision Summary for Module PD4

Electricity — what fun. This is definitely physics at its most grisly. The big problem with physics in general is that usually there's nothing to 'see'. You're told there's a current flowing, but there's nothing you can actually see with your eyes. That's what makes it so difficult. To get to grips with physics you have to get used to learning about things which you can't see. Try these questions and see how well you're doing. If you manage them then everything's just peachy. If you struggle at all, try them again after taking another squiz at the Module.

1) Describe what is meant by current, voltage and resistance.
   What units are they measured in?

2) How is current carried in metals?

3) What is an electrolyte? How is current carried in an electrolyte?

4) Describe the difference between AC and DC. What do their CRO traces look like?

5) Sketch the standard test circuit, with all the details. Describe how it's used.

6) Sketch a voltage-current graph for a resistor, wire, filament lamp and a diode.

7) How would you calculate the resistance from the graph?
   What does a curved graph indicate?

8) What happens when current flows through any resistor?

9) Find the voltage when a current of 0.5A flows through a resistance of 10Ω.

10) Scribble down eighteen circuit symbols that you know, with their names of course.

11) What are the properties of a diode? Give one example of where they're used.

12) How does the resistance of a light dependent resistor change as it gets darker?
    Give one use for them.

13) What is a thermistor? Give two examples of where they can be used.

14) What type of charge does an electron have?

15) What is static electricity? What is nearly always the cause of it building up?

16) Which particles move when static builds up, and which ones don't?

17) Describe how these machines use static electricity: a) inkjet printer b) photocopier.

18) Give one example of static being: a) a little joker   b) a terrorist.

19) How does earthing remove the excess charge on a body? What type of particle moves?

20) How would you calculate electrical power?

21) How can you calculate how much charge has passed in a certain time?

22) Sketch a diagram of a circuit to explain the formula $E = Q \times V$.

23) Write down any three formulae in formula triangles — it's good practice.

24) Find: a) The voltage when 0.5A flows through a resistance of 96Ω.

       b) The resistance of a kettle rated at 400W, drawing a current of 4A.

Magnetic Fields

There's a proper definition of a <u>magnetic field</u> which you really ought to learn:

> A <u>***MAGNETIC FIELD***</u> is a region where ***MAGNETIC MATERIALS*** (like iron and steel)
> and also ***WIRES CARRYING CURRENTS*** experience a ***FORCE*** acting on them.

Learn all These Magnetic Field Diagrams, Arrow-perfect

They're really likely to give you one of these diagrams to do in your Exam.
So make sure you know them, especially <u>which way the arrows point</u> — <u>always from North to South!</u>

Bar Magnet

Solenoid

Same field as
a bar magnet
<u>outside</u>.

<u>Strong and
uniform</u> field
on the <u>inside</u>.

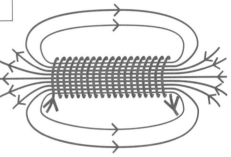

Two Bar Magnets Attracting

<u>Opposite poles attract</u>, as I'm sure you know.

Two Bar Magnets Repelling

<u>Like poles repel</u>, as you must surely know.

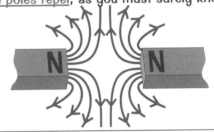

The Earth's Magnetic Field

Note that the
<u>magnetic poles</u>
are <u>opposite</u> to
the <u>geographic
poles</u>, ie. the
<u>south pole</u> is at
the <u>North Pole</u>
— if you see
what I mean!

The Magnetic Field Round a Current-carrying Wire

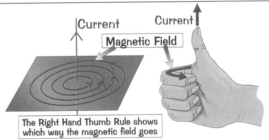

Current

Current

Magnetic Field

The Right Hand Thumb Rule shows
which way the magnetic field goes

A Plotting Compass is a Freely Suspended Magnet

1) This means it always <u>aligns itself</u> with the <u>magnetic field</u> that it's in.
2) This is great for plotting <u>magnetic field lines</u> like around the <u>bar magnets</u> shown above.
3) Away from any magnets, it will <u>align</u> with the magnetic field of the <u>Earth</u> and point <u>North</u>.
4) <u>Any magnet</u> suspended so it can turn <u>freely</u> will also come to rest pointing <u>North-South</u>.
5) The end of the magnet which points North is called a "<u>North-seeking pole</u>" or "<u>magnetic North</u>".
   The end pointing South will therefore be a "<u>magnetic South pole</u>". This is how they got their names.

Magnetic fields — there's no getting away from them...

Physicists often use the term <u>magnetic flux</u> — that's what's represented by the field lines.
More lines means a higher flux and a stronger magnet. Got that? Now, learn those six field
diagrams, and the details about the plotting compass. <u>Cover the page</u> and <u>scribble it all down</u>.

Electric Motors

Anything carrying a current in a magnetic field will experience a force.

A Current in a Magnetic Field Experiences a Force

The diagrams below demonstrate the force on a current-carrying wire placed in a magnetic field.
The force gets bigger if either the current or the magnetic field is made bigger.

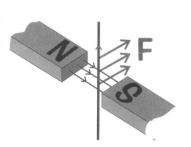

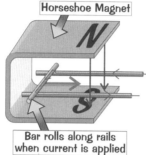

Horseshoe Magnet

Bar rolls along rails when current is applied

1) Note that in both cases the force on the wire is at 90° to both the wire and to the magnetic field.
2) You can always predict which way the force will act using Fleming's Left Hand Rule as shown below.
3) To experience the full force, the wire has to be at 90° to the magnetic field.
4) If the wire runs along the magnetic field it won't experience any force at all.
   At angles in between it'll feel some force.

The Simple Electric Motor

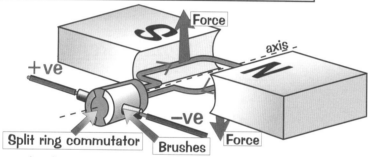

Force
axis
+ve
−ve
Force
Split ring commutator   Brushes

4 Factors which Speed it up

1) More **CURRENT**
2) More **TURNS** on the coil
3) **STRONGER MAGNETIC FIELD**
4) A **SOFT IRON CORE** in the coil

1) The diagram shows the forces acting on the two side arms of the coil.
2) These forces are just the usual forces which act on any current in a magnetic field.
3) Because the coil is on a spindle and the forces act one up and one down, it rotates.
4) The split ring commutator is a clever way of "swapping the contacts every half turn to keep the motor rotating in the same direction". Learn that statement because they might ask you.
5) The carbon brushes keep a good electrical contact while letting the commutator spin.
6) The direction of the motor can be reversed either by swapping the polarity of the DC supply or swapping the magnetic poles over.

Fleming's Left Hand Rule tells you Which way the Force Acts

1) They could test if you can do this, so practise it.
2) Using your left hand, point your First finger in the direction of the Field and your seCond finger in the direction of the Current.
3) Your thuMb will then point in the direction of the force (Motion).

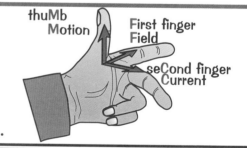

thuMb
Motion
First finger
Field
seCond finger
Current

Electric Motors are used in all sorts of Everyday Things

It's always handy to have a list of examples. Learn this lot so you can reel them off in the Exam: motors are used in things like vacuum cleaners, washing machines, tumble dryers, mixers, electric drills, and electric lawnmowers.

Fleming — how many broken wrists has he caused already...

Same old routine here. Learn all the details, diagrams and all, then cover the page and scribble it all down again from memory. You can scribble it as scruffy as you like — in pencil, biro, alphabetti-spaghetti, who cares — all you're trying to do is make sure that you really do know it.

The Dynamo Effect

The <u>dynamo effect</u> is another name for <u>electromagnetic induction</u>. Learn the definition spot on:

ELECTROMAGNETIC INDUCTION: The creation of a **_VOLTAGE_** (and maybe current) in a wire which is experiencing a **_CHANGE IN MAGNETIC FIELD_**.

For some reason they use the word '<u>induction</u>' rather than '<u>creation</u>', but it amounts to the <u>same thing</u>.

The Dynamo Effect — Move the Wire or the Magnet

<u>Electromagnetic induction</u> is the <u>induction</u> of a <u>voltage</u> and/or <u>current</u> in a conductor.
There are <u>two different situations</u> where you get <u>EM induction</u>. You need to know about <u>both</u> of them:
  a) The <u>conductor</u> moves across a <u>magnetic field</u> and '<u>cuts</u>' through the lines of <u>magnetic flux</u>.
  b) The <u>magnetic field</u> through a <u>closed coil</u> <u>changes</u>, ie. gets <u>bigger</u> or <u>smaller</u> or <u>reverses</u>.

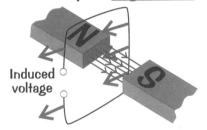 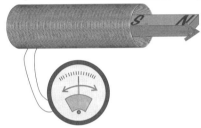 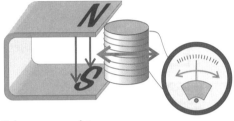

Induced voltage

If the direction of <u>movement</u> is <u>reversed</u>, then the <u>voltage/current</u> will be <u>reversed</u> too.

Four Factors Affect The Size of the Induced Voltage:

1) The **_STRENGTH_** of the **_MAGNET_**
2) The **_AREA_** of the **_COIL_**
3) The <u>number of</u> **_TURNS_** on the **_COIL_**
4) The **_SPEED_** of movement

These four factors can all be covered by <u>one statement</u>:

The size of the <u>INDUCED VOLTAGE</u> is proportional to the <u>RATE OF CHANGE OF FLUX</u> through the circuit.

Ideally, you should be able to see how <u>each one</u> of the four factors means <u>more flux is cut per second</u>. Ideally.

Generators and Dynamos

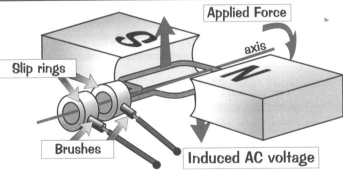

Applied Force

axis

Slip rings

Brushes

Induced AC voltage

<u>Dynamos</u> are slightly different from <u>generators</u> because they rotate the <u>magnet</u>. This still causes the <u>field</u> <u>through the coil</u> to <u>swap</u> every half turn, so the output is <u>just the same</u>, as shown in the CRO displays below.

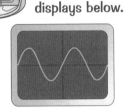 

1) Generators <u>rotate a coil</u> in a <u>magnetic field</u>.

2) Their <u>construction</u> is pretty much like a <u>motor</u>.

3) The <u>difference</u> is the <u>slip rings</u> and <u>carbon brushes</u> (made of carbon!). These replace the <u>split ring commutator</u>. In this set-up the contacts <u>don't swap</u> every half turn...

4) ...which means they produce <u>AC voltage</u>, as shown by the <u>CRO</u> <u>displays</u>. Note that <u>faster revs</u> produce not only <u>more peaks</u> but <u>higher overall voltage</u> too.

The Rate of Change of Flux — pretty tricky isn't it...

The dynamo effect gets my vote for "Definitely Most Trickiest Topic in GCSE Double Science". If it wasn't so important maybe you wouldn't have to bother learning it. The trouble is this is how all our electricity is generated. So it's pretty important. <u>Learn and scribble</u>...

Transformers

Transformers use Electromagnetic Induction. So they will only work on AC.

Transformers Change the Voltage — but only AC Voltages

Step-up transformers step the voltage up. They have more turns on the secondary coil.

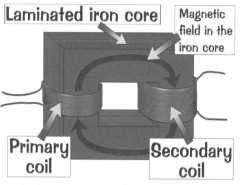

1) The laminated iron core is purely for transferring the magnetic flux from the primary coil to the secondary.

2) No electricity flows round the iron core, only magnetic flux.

3) The iron core is laminated with layers of insulation to reduce the eddy currents which heat it up, and therefore waste energy.

Step-down transformers step the voltage down. They have fewer turns on the secondary.

1) The primary coil produces magnetic flux (ie. a magnetic field) which stays within the iron core and this means it all passes through the secondary coil.

2) Because there is alternating current (AC) in the primary coil, this means that the magnetic flux in the iron core is reversing (50 times a second, usually) — ie. it is a changing flux.

3) This rapidly changing magnetic flux is then experienced by the secondary coil and this induces an alternating voltage in it — electromagnetic induction of a voltage in fact.

4) The relative number of turns on the two coils determines whether the voltage created in the secondary is greater or less than the voltage in the primary.

5) If you supplied DC to the primary, you'd get nothing out of the secondary at all. Sure, there'd still be flux in the iron core, but it wouldn't be constantly changing so there'd be no induction in the secondary because you need a changing flux to induce a voltage. Don't you! So don't forget it — transformers only work with AC. They won't work with DC at all.

Higher   Higher   Higher

The Transformer Equation — use it Either Way Up

In words: The RATIO OF TURNS on the two coils equals the RATIO OF THEIR VOLTAGES.

$$\frac{\text{Primary Voltage}}{\text{Secondary Voltage}} = \frac{\text{Number of turns on Primary}}{\text{Number of turns on Secondary}}$$

$$\frac{V_P}{V_S} = \frac{N_P}{N_S}$$

or

$$\frac{V_S}{V_P} = \frac{N_S}{N_P}$$

Well, it's just another formula. You stick in the numbers you've got and work out the one that's left. It's really useful to remember you can write it either way up — this example's much trickier algebra-wise if you start with V_S on the bottom...

EXAMPLE: A transformer has 40 turns on the primary and 800 on the secondary. If the input voltage is 1000 V find the output voltage.

ANSWER: $V_S/V_P = N_S/N_P$ so $V_S/1000 = 800/40$ $V_S = 1000 \times (800/40) = \underline{20,000\ V}$

There's also "Power In = Power Out" which gives "$V_P I_P = V_S I_S$"

This formula is true because transformers are nearly 100% efficient. But don't panic, it's just another formula — you stick numbers in and work out the bit that's left, and that's all there is to it. End of story.

The ubiquitous Iron Core — where would we be without it...

Besides their iron core, transformers have lots of other important details which also need to be learnt. You'll need to practise with those tricky equations too. They're unusual because they can't be put into formula triangles but other than that the method is the same. Just practise.

The National Grid

1) The National Grid is the network of pylons and cables which covers the whole country.
2) It takes electricity from the power stations to just where it's needed in homes and industry.
3) It enables power to be generated anywhere on the grid, and to then be supplied anywhere else on the grid.

All Power Stations are Pretty Much the Same

They all have a boiler of some sort, which makes steam which drives a turbine which drives a generator.
The generator produces electricity (by induction) by rotating an electromagnet within coils of wire (see P. 81).

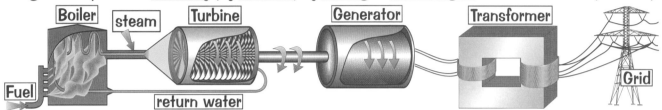

Learn all these features of the NATIONAL GRID — power stations, transformers, pylons, etc:

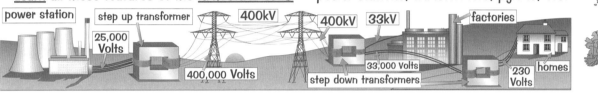

Most power stations are terribly inefficient — usually more than half the energy produced is wasted in the form of heat and noise. The efficiency of the power station depends a lot on the power source. Power sources include fossil fuels such as coal and gas, nuclear power, wind farms and HEP (hydroelectric power).

Pylon Cables are at 400,000 V to keep the Current Low

You need to understand why the voltage is so high and why it's AC. Learn these points:
1) The formula for power supplied is: Power = Voltage × Current or: $P = V \times I$
2) So to transmit a lot of power, you either need high voltage or high current.
3) The problem with high current is the loss (as heat) due to the resistance of the cables.
4) The formula for power loss due to resistance in the cables is: $P = I^2R$
5) Because of the I^2 bit, if the current is 10 times bigger, the losses will be 100 times bigger.

Higher

6) It's much cheaper to boost the voltage up to 400,000 V and keep the current very low so less energy is wasted.
7) This requires transformers as well as big pylons with huge insulators, but it's still cheaper.
8) The transformers have to step the voltage up at one end, for efficient transmission, and then bring it back down to safe useable levels at the other end.
9) This is why it has to be AC on the National Grid — so that the transformers will work!
10) Mains electricity in your house is AC 50 Hz — the voltage changes direction 50 times a second.

Efficiency Compares what you Get Out with what you Put In

A machine is a device which turns one type of energy into another.
The efficiency of any device is defined as:

$$\text{Efficiency} = \frac{\text{USEFUL Energy OUTPUT}}{\text{TOTAL Energy INPUT}}$$

$$\frac{\text{Energy out}}{\text{Efficiency} \times \text{Energy in}}$$

You can give efficiency as a fraction, decimal or percentage — eg. ¾ or 0.75 or 75%.

400,000 Volts? — that could give you a buzz...

Quite a few tricky details on this page. The power station and National Grid are easy enough, but fully explaining why pylon cables are at 400,000V is a bit trickier — but you do need to learn it. At least the bit on efficiency's simple enough — make sure you don't forget it though. Scribble it.

Work Done and Power

When a __force__ moves an __object__, energy is transferred and work is done.

That statement sounds far more complicated than it needs to. Try this:

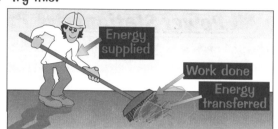

1) Whenever something <u>moves</u>, something else is providing some sort of <u>effort</u> to move it.
2) The thing putting the <u>effort</u> in needs a <u>supply of energy</u> (like <u>fuel</u> or <u>food</u> or <u>electricity</u> etc.).
3) It then does <u>work</u> by <u>moving</u> the object — and one way or another it <u>transfers the energy</u> it receives (as fuel) into <u>other forms</u>.
4) Whether this energy is transferred <u>usefully</u> (eg. by <u>lifting a load</u>) or is <u>wasted</u> (eg. lost as <u>friction</u>), you can still say that <u>work is done</u>. Just like Batman and Bruce Wayne, 'work done' and 'energy transferred' are indeed <u>one and the same</u>. (And they're both in <u>Joules</u>.)

It's Just Another Trivial Formula:

Work Done = Force × Distance

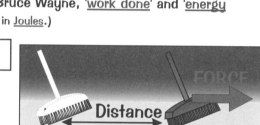

Whether the force is <u>friction</u> or <u>weight</u> or <u>tension in a rope</u>, it's always the same. To find how much <u>energy</u> has been <u>transferred</u> (in Joules), you just multiply the <u>force in N</u> by the <u>distance moved in m</u>. Easy as that. I'll show you...

__EXAMPLE__: Some hooligan kids drag an old tractor tyre 5m over rough ground. They pull with a total force of 340N. Find the energy transferred.
__ANSWER__: Wd = F×d = 340 × 5 = <u>1700J</u>.   Phew — easy peasy isn't it?

Power _is the Rate of Doing Work_ — ie. how much _per second_

Power is <u>not</u> the same thing as <u>force</u>, nor <u>energy</u>. A <u>powerful</u> machine is not necessarily one which can exert a strong <u>force</u> (though it usually ends up that way). A <u>powerful</u> machine is one which transfers <u>a lot of energy</u> in a <u>short space of time</u>. This is the <u>very easy formula</u> for power:

$$\text{Power} = \frac{\text{Work done}}{\text{Time taken}}$$

__EXAMPLE__: A motor transfers 4.8kJ of useful energy in 2 minutes. Find its power output.
__ANSWER__: P = Wd / t = 4,800 / 120 = 40W (or 40 J/s).
 (Note that the kJ had to be turned into J, and the minutes into seconds.)

Power _is Measured in Watts (or J/s)_

The proper unit of power is the <u>Watt</u>. <u>One Watt = 1 Joule of energy transferred per second</u>. <u>Power</u> means 'how much energy <u>per second</u>', so <u>Watts</u> are the same as '<u>Joules per second</u>' (J/s). Don't ever say 'watts per second' — it's <u>nonsense</u>.

Revise work done — what else...

'Energy transferred' and 'work done' are the same thing. I wonder how many times I need to say that before you'll remember. Power is '<u>work done divided by time taken</u>'. I wonder how many times you've got to see that before you realise you're supposed to <u>learn it</u> as well...

Kinetic Energy and Potential Energy

Kinetic Energy is Energy of Movement

Anything which is <u>moving</u> has <u>kinetic energy</u>.

There's a slightly <u>tricky formula</u> for it, so you have to concentrate a little bit <u>harder</u> for this one. But hey, that's life — it can be real tough sometimes:

Kinetic Energy = ½ × mass × velocity²

<u>EXAMPLE</u>: A car of mass 2450kg is travelling at 38m/s.
Calculate its kinetic energy.

<u>ANSWER</u>: It's pretty easy. You just plug the numbers into the formula but watch the v^2!
$KE = ½ m v^2 = ½ × 2450 × 38^2 = \underline{1\,768\,900J}$ (<u>Joules</u> because it's <u>energy</u>.)

(When the car stops suddenly, all this energy is dissipated as heat in the brakes — it's a lot of heat.)

Remember, the <u>kinetic energy</u> of something depends both on <u>mass</u> and <u>speed</u>.
The <u>more it weighs</u> and the <u>faster it's going</u>, the <u>bigger</u> its kinetic energy will be.

small mass, not fast
low kinetic energy

big fast lorries Ltd

big mass, real fast
high kinetic energy

Potential Energy is Energy Due to Height

The proper name for this kind of "<u>Potential Energy</u>" is <u>Gravitational Potential Energy</u>, (as opposed to "<u>elastic</u> potential energy" or "<u>chemical</u> potential energy"). The <u>higher up</u> something is, and the <u>more it weighs</u>, the bigger its gravitational potential energy.

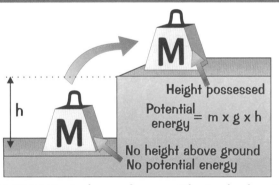

Height possessed
Potential energy = m x g x h

No height above ground
No potential energy

Potential Energy = mass × g × height

The proper name for g is '<u>gravitational field strength</u>'. On <u>Earth</u>, g is approximately <u>10m/s²</u>.

<u>EXAMPLE</u>: A sheep of mass 47kg is slowly raised through 6.3m.
Find the gain in potential energy.

<u>ANSWER</u>: It's even easier than before.
You just plug the numbers into the formula:
$PE = mgh = 47 × 10 × 6.3 = \underline{2961\ J}$
(<u>Joules</u> again because it's <u>energy</u> again.)

What do you call a sheep with no eyes and no legs?
Dunno?
A Cloud!

> Strictly speaking it's the <u>change</u> in potential energy we're dealing with, so the formula can sometimes be written as: <u>Change</u> in Potential Energy = mass × g × <u>change</u> in height. But that's a minor detail really, because it all works out just the same anyway.

Kinetic Energy — just get a move on and learn it, OK...

Phew! A couple of <u>tricky</u> formulae for you here. I mean, gosh, they've got more than three letters in them. Still, at least they fit into formula triangles, so you may still have some small chance of getting them right. Come on, I'm joking. Formulae are always a <u>doddle</u> aren't they?

K.E. and P.E. — Two Important Examples

1) Calculating Your Power Output

Both cases use the same formula:

$$POWER = \frac{ENERGY\ TRANSFERRED}{TIME\ TAKEN} \quad or \quad P = \frac{E}{t}$$

a) The Timed Run Upstairs:

In this case the <u>energy transferred</u> is simply the <u>potential energy you gain</u> (= mgh).
Hence   <u>Power = mgh/t</u>

Power output
= En. transferred/time
= mgh/t
= $(62 \times 10 \times 12) \div 14$
= <u>531W</u>

b) The Timed Acceleration:

This time the <u>energy transferred</u> is the <u>kinetic energy you gain</u> (= ½mv²).
Hence   <u>Power = ½mv²/t</u>

Power output
= En. transferred/time
= ½mv²/t
= $(½ \times 62 \times 8^2) \div 4$
= <u>496W</u>

2) Calculating the Speed of Falling Objects

When something falls, its <u>potential energy</u> is <u>converted</u> into <u>kinetic energy</u> (Principle of Conservation of Energy). Hence the <u>further</u> it falls, the <u>faster</u> it goes. In practice, some of the PE will be <u>dissipated</u> as <u>heat</u> due to <u>air resistance</u>, but in Exam questions they'll likely say you can <u>ignore</u> air resistance, in which case you'll just need to remember this <u>simple</u> and <u>really quite obvious</u> formula:

Kinetic energy gained = Potential Energy lost

<u>EXAMPLE</u>: A mouldy tomato of mass 140g is dropped from a height of 1.7m. Calculate its speed as it hits the floor.

<u>ANSWER</u>: There are four key steps to this method — and you've gotta learn them:

Step 1) Find the PE lost: = mgh = $0.14 \times 10 \times 1.7$ = <u>2.38J</u> — this must also be the KE gained.

Step 2) Equate the number of Joules of KE gained to the KE formula with v in, ' ½mv² ':

$$2.38 = ½mv^2$$

Step 3) Stick the numbers in: $2.38 = ½ \times 0.14 \times v^2$ or $2.38 = 0.07 \times v^2$
$$2.38 \div 0.07 = v^2 \quad so \quad v^2 = 34$$

Step 4) Square root: $v = \sqrt{34}$ = <u>5.83 m/s</u>

Easy peasy? Not really, no, but if you practise learning the four steps you'll find it's not too bad.

The Bouncing Ball — Same % Drop in Energy and Height

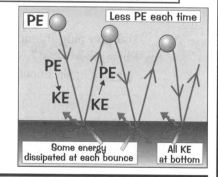

1) A <u>bouncing ball</u> is constantly <u>swapping</u> its energy <u>between PE and KE</u>, just as in the above example. As it <u>falls</u> it converts <u>PE into KE</u>. After the bounce, it <u>rises again</u> and converts its KE <u>back into PE</u>.

2) However, each time it <u>bounces</u> it will <u>lose</u> some energy in the bounce. This means it'll leave the surface a bit <u>slower</u> than it hits it, which means with <u>less KE</u>, so it <u>won't reach the same height</u> as the previous bounce.

3) The relation between <u>total energy</u> and <u>height reached</u> is really simple: If the ball <u>loses</u> say <u>10%</u> of its energy <u>each bounce</u>, then the <u>height reached</u> will also be <u>10% lower</u> each time. It's as simple as that.

Revise falling objects — just don't lose your grip...

This is it. This is the zenith of GCSE Physics. This is the nearest it gets to <u>real</u> Physics (A-level). Look at that terrifying square root sign for a start — and a four step method. It's scary stuff.

Digital and Analogue Signals

Analogue and Digital signals are pretty important — life would be pretty dull without them — no phones, no computers. Even groovy digital watches wouldn't exist.

Analogue *Varies* But Digital's *Either On or Off*

1) Analogue and digital signals are very different.

2) An analogue wave can take any value within a certain range. (Remember: analogue — any.)

3) A digital signal on the other hand can only take two values — on or off.

4) The two values of a digital signal are sometimes given other names — but the point is that there are only two possible values.

These other names might be...
...true or false, 1 or 0, high or low etc.

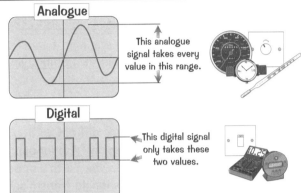

This analogue signal takes every value in this range.

This digital signal only takes these two values.

Signals Have to Be Amplified

Both digital and analogue signals weaken as they travel — so they need to be amplified along their route. They also pick up random disturbances, called noise.

Digital Signals are Far Better Quality

1) Noise is less of a problem with digital signals. If you receive a noisy digital signal, it's pretty obvious what it's supposed to be.

2) But if you receive a noisy analogue signal, it's difficult to know what the original signal would have looked like.

This noisy digital signal... ...is obviously supposed to be this.

But this noisy analogue signal... ...could have started like this... ...or this...

3) This is why digital signals are much higher quality — the information received is the same as the original.

4) It's also much quicker to send information as a digital signal than as an analogue signal. This means that in the same time, you can send loads more information if you use digital signals.

5) Also, many digital signals can be transmitted at once by a clever way of overlapping them on the same cable or EM wave — but you don't need to learn *how* they do it. Phew.

Analogue can be *Converted to Digital and Back Again*

Higher — Higher

1) Modems convert digital signals into analogue ones and vice-versa.

2) Signals from a computer are digital, but phone lines work on analogue signals — so they have to be converted from one form to the other. Modems contain a DAC (digital to analogue converter) — this produces a signal that can travel down a phone line.

3) They also contain an ADC (analogue to digital converter) so the modem at the other end of the line can convert the signal back into digital form. You don't have to know how they work, but they're very clever things.

Higher — Higher

Read the signals — learn this stuff right now...

Make sure you know the difference between digital and analogue signals, and why digital ones are better. Learn that little bit on ADCs and DACs as well, while you're at it. And when you think you know it all, cover the page, scribble it all down, and see what you got right.

EM Waves for Communication

Most of this stuff you should recognise from <u>PD1</u> — if you can cast your mind back that far.
If there's anything you're not sure of, <u>go back and check it</u>.
<u>Electromagnetic (EM) waves</u> can be used to <u>communicate information</u>. Being <u>waves</u>, they can be
<u>reflected</u>, <u>refracted</u> and <u>diffracted</u> — which is either useful or a pain in the neck, it all depends.

EM Waves can Carry Information

<u>Radio</u>, <u>microwaves</u>, <u>infra-red</u> and <u>light</u> can all carry <u>information</u>.

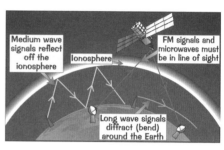

1) <u>Radio waves</u> are used mainly for <u>communication</u>. Both <u>TV</u> and
<u>FM radio</u> use short, <u>1m</u> wavelength waves. To receive these
wavelengths you need to be in <u>direct sight</u> of the <u>transmitter</u>,
because they don't bend (diffract) very much. <u>Long wave</u> radio
waves (1km wavelength) will <u>diffract</u> to bend around the Earth.
<u>Medium</u> wave signals <u>reflect off the ionosphere</u>, which is an
electrically charged layer in the Earth's upper atmosphere.

2) <u>Microwaves</u> are used for <u>satellite transmissions</u>. They use frequencies that <u>pass easily</u> through the
Earth's atmosphere, including <u>clouds</u>. Microwaves are also used in radar.

3) <u>Infra-red</u> is used for <u>remote control</u> of <u>TVs and videos</u>. It's ideal for sending <u>harmless signals</u> over
<u>short distances</u>. It's also used for <u>telecommunications</u> and <u>computer links</u>. The IR is transmitted
down <u>fibre optic cables</u> in digitally coded pulses.

4) <u>Light</u> transmits optical information all the time — that's the only reason you can read this.

Optical Fibres — Communications and Endoscopes

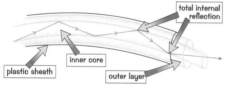

1) <u>Optical fibres</u> carry <u>information</u> by <u>total internal reflections</u>.
2) The fibre must be <u>narrow enough</u> to keep the angles <u>above
the critical angle</u>, so the fibre mustn't be bent <u>too sharply</u>
anywhere.

An <u>endoscope</u> uses fibre optics to look inside people. It's a <u>narrow
bunch</u> of <u>optical fibres</u> with a <u>lens system</u> at each end. Another bunch
of optical fibres carries light down <u>inside</u> to see with.
The image is displayed as a <u>full colour moving image</u> on a TV screen.
This means they can do operations <u>without</u> cutting big holes in people.

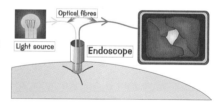

Satellites Can be Used for Global Communications

1) The <u>microwave signal</u> is <u>transmitted</u> upwards into space by a ground station transmitter dish in
one part of the world.
2) The signal is picked up by the <u>satellite receiver dish</u> orbiting hundreds of km <u>above the Earth</u>.
3) The satellite <u>transmits</u> the signal back to Earth in a different direction...
4) ...where it's then received by another ground dish in <u>another part</u> of the world.

Refraction and Diffraction Can Affect Communication

1) EM waves travel at <u>different speeds</u> in the different layers of the
Earth's atmosphere.
2) Microwaves may <u>refract</u> at the <u>boundaries</u> between the different layers.
3) This can <u>disrupt</u> the signal as it bends <u>away</u> from the receiver dish.
4) <u>Diffraction</u> can also occur at the <u>edges</u> of transmission dishes
— the waves <u>spread out</u>, which can also result in <u>signal loss</u>.

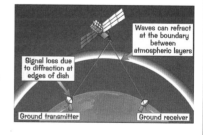

Learn about satellites — and look down on your friends...

That's just a quick reminder of some of that EM spectrum stuff, so make sure you can
remember all the details. The bit on satellite systems is new, so try writing yourself a
<u>mini-essay</u> on that. As for the rest of it — it should be easy, but make sure you know it.

Higher Higher Higher Higher Higher Higher

Revision Summary for Module PD5

It's an outrage — just so much you've gotta learn. It's all work, work, work, no time to rest, no time to play. But then that's the grim, cruel reality of life in 21st Century Britain — just drudgery, hard work and untold dreariness. "And then he woke up and it had all been a dream..." Yeah, maybe life's not so bad after all — even for hard-done-by teenagers. Just a few jolly bits and bobs to learn in warm, cosy, comfortable civilisation. Practise these questions over and over again till you can answer them all effortlessly. Smile and enjoy.

1) Describe what's meant by a magnetic field.

2) Sketch magnetic fields for: a) a bar magnet   b) a solenoid   c) two bar magnets attracting   d) two bar magnets repelling   e) the Earth's magnetic field   f) a current-carrying wire

3) Sketch two pictures to show a current carrying wire experiencing a force in a magnetic field.

4) Sketch an electric motor and list the 4 factors which speed it up.

5) What is a split ring commutator and why is it used?

6) What do you use Fleming's Left Hand Rule for? Which direction do your fingers point in?

7) List 6 everyday items that use electric motors.

8) Give the definition of electromagnetic induction. Sketch three cases where it happens.

9) List the four factors which affect the size of the induced voltage.

10) Sketch a generator, labelling all the parts. Describe how it works and what all the bits do.

11) Write down how a dynamo works.

12) Sketch the two types of transformer and highlight the main details.

13) Explain how a transformer works. Why is the iron core laminated?

14) Write down the transformer equation. Do your own worked example — it's ace practice.

15) Sketch a typical power station, and the National Grid, and explain why it's at 400 kV.

16) Write down the formula for calculating efficiency.

17) What's the connection between 'work done' and 'energy transferred'?

18) What's the formula for work done? A crazy dog drags a big branch 12m over the next-door neighbour's front lawn, pulling with a force of 535N. How much energy was transferred?

19) What's the formula for power? What are the units of power?

20) An electric motor uses 540kJ of electrical energy in 4½ minutes. What is its power consumption?

21) Write down the formulae for KE and PE. Find the KE of a 78kg sheep moving at 23m/s.

22) Calculate the power output of a 78kg sheep which runs up a 20m staircase in 16.5 seconds.

23) Calculate the speed of a 78kg sheep as it hits the floor after falling from a height of 20m.

24) If the sheep bounces back up to a height of 18m calculate the % loss of KE at the bounce.

25) Describe the differences between digital and analogue signals. Give 3 examples of each.

26) Describe analogue and digital signals. Why are digital signals better? What are ADCs and DACs?

27) Describe how radio waves with different frequencies travel from transmitter to receiver.

28) How do optical fibres work? Give details of one use of optical fibres.

29) Explain how satellites are used in global communications.

30) Describe two ways in which signals can be lost from satellite transmissions.

Basic Mechanics

Speed, Velocity and Acceleration

1) <u>Speed and velocity</u> are both measured in <u>m/s</u> (or km/h or mph), but there's <u>a subtle difference</u>:

<u>Speed</u> is just <u>how fast</u> you're going (eg. 40m/s) with no regard to the direction.

<u>Velocity</u> however must <u>also</u> have the <u>direction</u> specified, eg. 40m/s, 060°.

The Speed / Velocity Formula

$$\text{Speed} = \frac{\text{Distance}}{\text{Time}}$$

2) <u>Acceleration</u> is <u>definitely not</u> the same as <u>velocity</u> or <u>speed</u>. Acceleration involves a <u>change</u> in either <u>speed</u> or <u>direction</u>.

The Acceleration Formula

$$\text{Acceleration} = \frac{\text{Change in Velocity}}{\text{Time Taken}}$$

3) So acceleration is the '<u>velocity change per unit time</u>'.
4) The <u>units</u> of acceleration are <u>m/s^2</u>. <u>Not m/s</u>, which is <u>velocity</u>, but <u>m/s^2</u>.

Newton's Three Laws of Motion

1) **Newton's First Law:** If the <u>forces</u> on an object are all <u>balanced</u> then:
   (i) If it's <u>stationary</u>, it'll just <u>stay still</u>.
   (ii) If it's <u>already moving</u>, it'll keep moving with the <u>same velocity</u>.

forces balance, so steady speed

2) **Newton's Second Law:** An <u>unbalanced force</u> always produces an <u>acceleration</u> (or deceleration).
3) This 'acceleration' results in the object <u>starting to move</u>, <u>stopping</u>, <u>speeding up</u>, <u>slowing down</u> or <u>changing direction</u>.
4) The <u>formula</u> relating <u>force (F)</u>, <u>mass (m)</u> and <u>acceleration (a)</u> is:

unbalanced forces, so accelerating

$$\mathbf{F = ma} \quad \text{or} \quad \mathbf{a = F/m}$$

5) **Newton's Third Law:** If an object A <u>exerts a force</u> on an object B, then object B exerts <u>the exact opposite force</u> on object A.
6) This means, for example, that if you <u>push against a wall</u>, the wall will <u>push back</u> against you, <u>just as hard</u>. And as soon as you <u>stop</u> pushing, <u>so does the wall</u>.

Higher

Gravity is the Force of Attraction Between All Masses

1) <u>Gravity</u> attracts <u>all masses</u>, but you only notice it when one of the masses is <u>really big</u>, eg. the Earth.
2) On Earth, gravity makes all things <u>accelerate</u> towards the <u>centre of the planet</u> with the <u>same acceleration</u>, g, equal to <u>10 m/s^2</u>. (g is <u>constant</u> and sometimes called the <u>acceleration of free fall</u>.)
3) <u>Weight</u> is not the same as mass. Weight is a <u>force</u> and is measured in <u>Newtons</u>. Mass is <u>not</u> a force and is measured in <u>kilograms</u>.
4) Weight is caused by the <u>pull of gravity</u> on a mass. A 1 kg mass has the <u>same mass</u> whether it's on Earth or on the Moon, but it will <u>weigh less</u> on the Moon than it does on Earth because the force of gravity pulling on it is <u>smaller</u>.
5) There is a very <u>important formula</u> relating <u>weight</u>, <u>mass</u> and <u>gravity</u>: ➡

$$\mathbf{W = m \times g}$$

(Weight = mass × g)

Objects in Free-Fall Reach a Terminal Velocity

1) When a free-falling object <u>first sets off</u> it has <u>much more</u> force <u>accelerating</u> it than <u>air resistance</u> slowing it down.
2) As its <u>speed</u> increases the resistance <u>builds up</u>. This gradually <u>reduces</u> the <u>acceleration</u> until eventually the <u>resistance force</u> is <u>equal</u> to the <u>accelerating force</u>.
3) When the forces balance, it doesn't accelerate any more and has reached its <u>terminal velocity</u>.

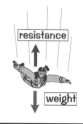
resistance

weight

Come on — it's not rocket science...

Basic mechanics is covered in Module <u>PD3</u> as well, so this should be revision. But make sure you know it because they can ask about acceleration and velocity in the Exam questions about <u>space</u>.

The Planets

You need to revise the <u>order</u> of the planets, which is made easier by using the little jollyism below:

Mercury,	Venus,	Earth,	Mars,	(Asteroids),	Jupiter,	Saturn,	Uranus,	Neptune,	Pluto
(My	Very	Energetic	Maiden	Aunt	Just	Swam	Under	North	Pier)

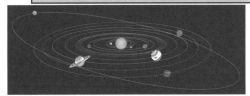

Mercury, <u>Venus</u>, <u>Earth</u> and <u>Mars</u> are known as the <u>inner planets</u>.
<u>Jupiter</u>, <u>Saturn</u>, <u>Uranus</u>, <u>Neptune</u> and <u>Pluto</u> are much further away and are the <u>outer planets</u>.

Planets Reflect Sunlight and Orbit in Ellipses

1) You can <u>see</u> some of the nearer planets with the <u>naked eye</u> at night, eg. Mars and Venus.
2) They look just like <u>stars</u>, but they are of course <u>totally different</u>.
3) Stars are <u>huge</u> and <u>very far away</u> and <u>give out</u> lots of light.
   The planets are <u>smaller</u> and <u>nearer</u> and they just <u>reflect sunlight</u> falling on them.
4) The Sun, like other stars, produces <u>heat</u> from <u>nuclear fusion reactions</u> which turn <u>hydrogen</u> into <u>helium</u>. It gives out the <u>full spectrum</u> of <u>EM radiation</u>.
5) Planets always orbit around <u>stars</u>. In our Solar System the planets orbit the <u>Sun</u> of course.
6) These orbits are all <u>slightly elliptical</u> (elongated circles), as are the orbits of moons around planets.
7) All the planets in our Solar System orbit in the <u>same plane</u> except Pluto (as shown in the pic above).
8) The <u>further</u> the planet is from the Sun, the <u>longer</u> its orbit takes (see below about gravity).

Gravity Decreases Quickly as you get Further Away

1) With <u>very large</u> masses like <u>stars</u> and <u>planets</u>, gravity is <u>very big</u> and acts <u>a long way out</u>.
2) The <u>closer</u> you get to a star or a planet, the <u>stronger</u> the <u>force of attraction</u>.
3) To <u>counteract</u> the stronger gravity, planets nearer the Sun move <u>faster</u> and cover their orbit <u>quicker</u>.
4) <u>Comets</u> are also held in <u>orbit</u> by gravity, as are <u>moons</u> and <u>satellites</u> and <u>space stations</u>.
5) The size of the force of gravity follows the fairly famous 'inverse square' relationship.
   The main effect of that is that the force <u>decreases very quickly</u> with increasing <u>distance</u>.
   The <u>formula</u> is $F \propto 1/d^2$, but I reckon it's <u>easier</u> just to remember the basic idea <u>in words</u>:

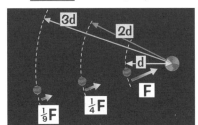

a) If you <u>double the distance</u> from a planet, the size of the <u>force</u> will <u>decrease</u> by a <u>factor of four</u> (2^2).

b) If you <u>treble the distance</u>, the <u>force</u> of gravity will <u>decrease</u> by a <u>factor of nine</u> (3^2), and so on.

c) On the other hand, if you get <u>twice as close</u> the gravity becomes <u>four times stronger</u>.

Centripetal Forces mean Elliptical Orbits

1) A <u>centripetal force</u> is one that attracts things towards a <u>single point</u>, and keeps things moving in <u>elliptical or circular orbits</u>.

2) The Sun's <u>gravity</u> provides the centripetal force needed to keep <u>planets</u> and <u>comets</u> in their orbits.

3) They are continually <u>pulled</u> towards the Sun, which stops them just flying off into space.

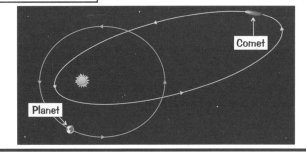

If you're gonna revise properly you'd better planet first...

Isn't the Solar System great! All those pretty coloured planets and all that big black empty space. You can look forward to one or two easy questions on the planets — or you might get two real horrors instead. Be ready, <u>learn</u> all the <u>fiddly little details</u> till you know it all real good.

Moons, Meteorites, Asteroids and Comets

Moons are Heavenly Bodies Which Orbit Planets

1) The Earth only has <u>one</u> moon of course, but some of the <u>other planets</u> have <u>quite a few</u>.

2) We can only <u>see</u> the moon because it <u>reflects sunlight</u>.

3) The <u>phases of the moon</u> happen depending on <u>how much</u> of the <u>illuminated side</u> of the moon we can <u>see</u>, as shown:

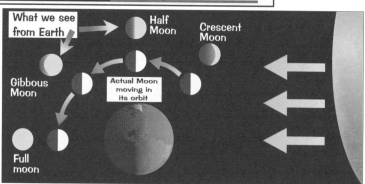

Asteroids are a Belt of Rocks Orbiting Between Mars and Jupiter

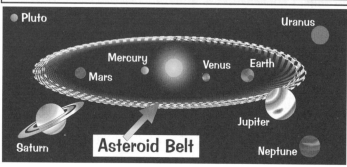

1) There are <u>several thousand</u> lumps of <u>rock</u> orbiting the Sun in a <u>belt</u> between the orbits of <u>Mars</u> and <u>Jupiter</u>.

2) They <u>vary in size</u> from about <u>1,000 km</u> diameter down to just <u>1 km</u>.

3) These <u>asteroids</u> usually <u>stay in their orbits</u> but if they <u>collide</u> and get <u>knocked out</u> of their orbits they become <u>meteorites</u>...

Meteorites are Lumps of Rock that Crash Down to Earth

1) Don't confuse <u>meteorites</u> with <u>asteroids</u>.

2) <u>Asteroids</u> stay in a <u>nice steady orbit</u> round the Sun.

3) <u>Meteorites</u> are asteroids that get <u>knocked out</u> of their nice steady orbit and then <u>collide with Earth</u>.

4) When they enter the <u>Earth's atmosphere</u> they <u>burn up</u>, and we then see them as <u>shooting stars</u>.

5) If they're <u>big enough</u>, they reach the <u>Earth's surface</u>. This is <u>rare</u>, but it's <u>serious</u> when they do.

Comets Orbit the Sun, but have very Eccentric (elongated) Orbits

1) <u>Comets</u> only appear <u>every few years</u> because their <u>orbits</u> take them <u>very far from the Sun</u> and then <u>back in close</u>, which is when <u>we</u> see them.

2) The Sun is <u>not at the centre</u> of the orbit but <u>near one end</u> as shown.

3) Comet <u>orbits</u> can be in <u>different planes</u> from the orbits of the planets.

4) Comets are made of <u>ice</u> and <u>rock</u> and, as they approach the Sun, the <u>ice melts</u>, leaving a <u>bright tail</u> of <u>debris</u> which can be <u>millions of km</u> long.

5) The comet travels <u>much faster</u> when it's <u>nearer the Sun</u> than it does when it's in the more <u>distant</u> part of its orbit.
This is because the <u>pull of gravity</u> makes it <u>speed up</u> as it gets <u>closer</u>, and then <u>slows it down</u> as it gets <u>further away</u> from the Sun.

Learn about these lumps of rock — and watch out for them...

Four more cosmic bits and bobs for you to know about. There's more to a Solar System than just planets you know. Make sure you learn all the details about these different lumps of rock. It's all in the syllabus, so they could ask you about any of it. Four <u>mini-essays</u> please. Now.

The Universe

The Sun is Huge Compared to the Earth

1) The Sun is a star and is <u>much larger</u> than the Earth.
In theory, the Earth could fit inside the Sun 1.3 million times!
2) The Earth is about <u>150 million kilometres</u> away from the Sun.
The next nearest star to the Earth is more than <u>250,000</u> times further away.
3) <u>Comets</u> are much <u>smaller</u> than planets — they usually have a diameter of just a few kilometres.
4) <u>Meteorites</u> are smaller still. The vast majority are no more than a few <u>metres</u> across (when they set off) and they <u>burn up</u> completely before they reach the ground. Occasionally there are <u>really big</u> ones which do hit the Earth.

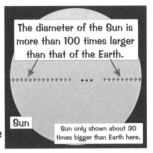

The diameter of the Sun is more than 100 times larger than that of the Earth.

Sun

Sun only shown about 30 times bigger than Earth here.

Our Sun is in The Milky Way Galaxy

1) The <u>Sun</u> is one of <u>many millions</u> of <u>stars</u> which form the <u>Milky Way Galaxy</u>.
2) The <u>distance</u> between neighbouring stars is usually <u>millions of times greater</u> than the distance between <u>planets</u> in our Solar System.
3) <u>Gravity</u> is of course the <u>force</u> which keeps the stars <u>together</u> in a <u>galaxy</u> and, like most things in the Universe, the <u>galaxies all rotate</u>, kinda like a catherine wheel only <u>much slower</u>.
4) Our Sun is out towards the <u>end</u> of one of the <u>spiral arms</u> of the Milky Way galaxy.

You are here

You are here

The Whole Universe has More Than A Billion Galaxies

1) <u>Galaxies</u> themselves are often <u>millions of times further apart</u> than the <u>stars are</u> within a galaxy.
2) So even the slowest amongst you will soon begin to realise that the Universe is <u>mostly empty space</u> and is <u>really really big</u>. Have you ever been to Wembley? Yeah? Well, it's even bigger than that.

Black Holes Don't Let Anything Escape

1) The gravity on neutron stars, white dwarfs and black dwarfs (see p.96) is <u>so strong</u> that it <u>crushes atoms</u>. The stuff in the stars gets <u>squashed up</u> so much that they're <u>MILLIONS OF TIMES DENSER</u> than anything on Earth.
2) If <u>enough</u> matter is left behind after a supernova explosion, it's <u>so dense</u> that <u>nothing</u> can escape the powerful gravitational field. Not even electromagnetic waves. The dead star is then called a <u>black hole</u>.
3) Even though black holes are formed from massive stars, they usually have a diameter of only a few <u>kilometres</u>.
4) Black holes <u>aren't visible</u> because any light being emitted is sucked right back in there (that's why it's called 'black', d'oh).
5) Astronomers can detect black holes in other ways — they can observe <u>X-rays</u> emitted by <u>hot gases</u> from other stars as they spiral into the black hole.

Galaxies, Milky Way — shove that down yer black hole...

More gripping facts about the Universe. Just look at those numbers: there's <u>millions</u> of stars in the Milky Way, the universe contains <u>billions</u> of galaxies, all <u>millions</u> of times further apart than 100,000 light years... Doesn't it just blow your socks off...

The Origin of the Universe

The <u>Big Bang Theory</u> of the Universe is the <u>most convincing</u> at the present time.

Red-shift and Background Radiation need Explaining

There are <u>three important bits of evidence</u> you need to know about:

1) Light From Other Galaxies is Red-Shifted

1) When we look at <u>light from distant galaxies</u> we find that <u>all the frequencies</u> are <u>shifted</u> towards the <u>red end</u> of the spectrum.

2) In other words, the <u>frequencies</u> are all <u>slightly lower</u> than they should be. It's the same effect as a car <u>horn</u> sounding lower-pitched when the car is travelling <u>away</u> from you. The sound <u>drops in frequency</u>.

3) This is called the <u>Doppler effect</u>.

4) <u>Measurements</u> of the red-shift suggest that <u>all the galaxies</u> are <u>moving away from us</u> very quickly — and it's the <u>same result</u> whichever direction you look.

2) The Further Away a Galaxy is, the Greater the Red-Shift

1) <u>More distant</u> galaxies have <u>greater</u> red-shifts than nearer ones.

2) This means that more distant galaxies are <u>moving away faster</u> than nearer ones.

3) The inescapable <u>conclusion</u> appears to be that the whole Universe is <u>expanding</u>.

1) You can use a <u>balloon</u> to try and picture the <u>expanding universe</u>.

2) Blow up the balloon until it's <u>just inflated</u> and then draw some '<u>galaxies</u>' on it.

3) Continue blowing until the balloon is <u>noticeably larger</u>.

4) The 'galaxies' are now <u>further apart</u> than they were.

5) The <u>further apart</u> two 'galaxies' were from each other in the first place, the <u>more</u> they seem to have moved apart.

6) Galaxies that start off further apart move farther <u>IN THE SAME TIME</u>, which means they <u>MOVE FASTER</u>.

7) This is just like the <u>real galaxies</u> in the expanding universe.

3) There's a Uniform Microwave Radiation From All Directions

1) This <u>low frequency radiation</u> comes from <u>all directions</u> and from <u>all parts</u> of the Universe.

2) It's known as the <u>background radiation</u> (of the Big Bang). It's nothing to do with radioactive background radiation on Earth.

3) For complicated reasons this background radiation is <u>strong evidence</u> for an <u>initial Big Bang</u>, and as the Universe <u>expands and cools</u>, so this background radiation "<u>cools</u>" and <u>drops in frequency</u>.

The Big Bang — it's explosive stuff...

Let's get this straight. The <u>galaxies</u>, which are already squillions of miles apart, are getting <u>further and further apart</u> even as we speak! Geesch — it's enough to make you feel lonely. Try not to worry about it too much and get on with <u>learning</u> this page. <u>Scribblin'</u> time...

The Origin and Future of the Universe

The Big Bang Theory — Well Popular

1) Since all the galaxies appear to be <u>moving apart</u> very rapidly, the <u>obvious conclusion</u> is that there was an <u>initial explosion</u>: the <u>Big Bang</u>.

2) All the matter in the Universe must have been <u>compressed into a very small space</u> and then it <u>exploded</u> and the <u>expansion</u> is still going on.

3) The Big Bang is believed to have happened around <u>15 billion years ago</u>.

4) The age of the Universe can be <u>estimated</u> from the <u>current rate of expansion</u>.

5) These estimates are <u>not very accurate</u> because it's hard to tell how much the expansion has <u>slowed down</u> since the Big Bang.

6) The rate at which the expansion is <u>slowing down</u> is an <u>important factor</u> in deciding the <u>future</u> of the Universe.

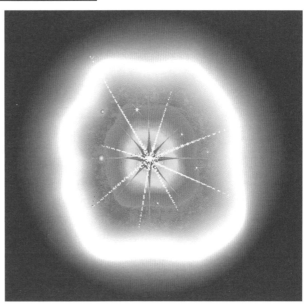

7) <u>Without gravity</u> the Universe would expand at the <u>same rate forever</u>.

8) However, the <u>attraction</u> between all the mass in the Universe tends to <u>slow</u> the expansion down.

The Future of the Universe:

It Could Expand Forever — or Collapse into The Big Crunch

1) The eventual fate of the Universe depends on <u>how fast</u> the galaxies are <u>moving apart</u> and how much <u>total mass</u> there is in it.

2) We can <u>measure</u> how fast the galaxies are <u>separating</u> quite easily, but we'd also like to know just <u>how much mass</u> there is in the Universe in order to <u>predict the future</u> of it.

3) This is proving <u>tricky</u> as most of the mass appears to be <u>invisible</u>, eg. <u>black holes</u>, <u>big planets</u>, <u>interstellar dust</u> etc.

Anyway, depending on <u>how much mass</u> there is, there are <u>two ways</u> the Universe could go:

1) Le Crunch — But Only if there's Enough Mass

If there's <u>enough mass</u> compared with <u>how fast</u> the galaxies are currently moving, the Universe will eventually <u>stop expanding</u> and <u>begin contracting</u>. This would end in a <u>Big Crunch</u>. The Big Crunch could be followed by another Big Bang and then <u>endless cycles</u> of <u>expansion and contraction</u>.

2) If there's Too Little Mass — then it's Le Miserable Eternity

If there's <u>too little mass</u> in the Universe to slow the expansion down, then it could <u>expand forever</u> with the Universe becoming <u>more and more spread out</u> into eternity. This seems <u>way too dismal</u> for my liking. I much prefer the idea of the Universe going <u>endlessly in cycles</u>.
But what was there <u>before</u> the Universe? Or what is there <u>outside</u> of it? It's <u>mindboggling</u>.

Time and Space — it's funny old stuff isn't it...

I think it's great that they've put all this stuff on space in the syllabus. I mean wow, something in Physics that's actually interesting. The great thing about learning a few bits and bobs about the Universe is that it can make you sound really clever when you tell people about it. "Ah well, it's all to do with the diminishing Doppler red-shift over the last 15 billion years", you can say.

The Life Cycle of Stars

Stars go through many traumatic stages in their lives — just like teenagers.

Clouds of Dust and Gas

1) Stars initially form from clouds of **DUST AND GAS**.

Protostar

2) The force of gravity makes the dust particles come spiralling in together. As they do, gravitational energy is converted into heat energy and the temperature rises.

3) When the temperature gets high enough, hydrogen nuclei undergo nuclear fusion to form helium nuclei and give out massive amounts of heat and light. A star is born. It immediately enters a long stable period where the heat created by the nuclear fusion provides an outward pressure to balance the force of gravity pulling everything inwards.
In this stable period it's called a **MAIN SEQUENCE STAR** and it lasts about 10 billion years. (The Sun is in the middle of this stable period — or to put it another way, the Earth has already had half its innings before the Sun engulfs it!)

Main Sequence Star

Red Giant

4) Eventually the hydrogen begins to run out and the star then swells into a **RED GIANT**. It becomes red because the surface cools.

5) A small star like our Sun will then begin to cool and contract into a **WHITE DWARF** and then finally, as the light fades completely, it becomes a **BLACK DWARF**. (That's going to be really sad.)

Small stars

White Dwarf

Black Dwarf

Big stars

6) Big stars however, start to glow brightly again as they undergo more fusion and expand and contract several times forming heavier elements in various nuclear reactions. Eventually they'll explode in a **SUPERNOVA**.

new planetary nebula... ...and a new solar system

Supernova

Neutron Star...

...or Black Hole

7) The exploding supernova throws the outer layers of dust and gas into space leaving a very dense core called a **NEUTRON STAR**. If the star is big enough this will become a **BLACK HOLE**.

8) The dust and gas thrown off by the supernova will form into **SECOND GENERATION STARS** like our Sun. The heavier elements are only made in the final stages of a big star just before the final supernova. That means that the presence of heavier elements in the Sun and the inner planets is clear evidence that our beautiful and wonderful world, with its warm sunsets and fresh morning dews, has all formed out of the snotty remains of a grisly old star's last dying sneeze.

9) The matter from which neutron stars and white dwarfs and black dwarfs are made is **MILLIONS OF TIMES DENSER** than any matter on Earth because the gravity is so strong it even crushes the atoms.

Twinkle Twinkle little star, How I wond.. — JUST LEARN IT PAL...

Erm. Just how do they know all that? As if it's not outrageous enough that they reckon to know the whole history of the Earth for the last five billion years, they also reckon to know the whole life cycle of stars, when they're all billions and billions of km away. It's just an outrage.

Searching for Life on Other Planets

There's a good chance that life exists somewhere else in the Universe.
Scientists use <u>three methods</u> to search for anything from amoebas to little green men.

1) SETI Looks for Radio Signals from Other Planets

1) Us Earthlings are constantly beaming <u>radio</u>, <u>TV</u> and <u>radar</u> into space for any passing aliens to detect. There might be life out there that's as clever as we are. Or even more clever. They may have built <u>transmitters</u> to send out signals like ours.

2) <u>SETI</u> stands for "Search for Extra Terrestrial Intelligence". Scientists on the SETI project are looking for <u>narrow bands</u> of <u>radio wavelengths</u> coming to Earth from outer space. They're looking for <u>meaningful signals</u> in all the '<u>noise</u>'.

3) Signals on a narrow band can <u>only</u> come from a <u>transmitter</u>. The 'noise' comes from giant stars and gas clouds.

4) It takes <u>ages</u> to analyse all the radio waves so the SETI folk get help from the public — you can download a <u>screen saver</u> off the internet which analyses a chunk of radio waves.

5) SETI has been going for the last <u>40 years</u> but they've <u>not found anything</u>. Not a sausage. ☹

6) Astronomers have also been searching for other <u>stars</u> with <u>planets</u> orbiting them. Sounds like a sensible place to look I suppose...

2) Robots Collect Photos and Samples

This <u>could</u> be a microscopic fossil of a bacteria-like organism from Mars... Then again, it could be a crystal, bits of metal, or the remains of last night's curry. 500 nm

1) Scientists have sent robots in spacecraft to <u>Mars</u> and <u>Europa</u> (one of Jupiter's moons) to look for microorganisms.

2) The robots wander round the planet, sending <u>photographs</u> back to Earth or <u>collecting samples</u> for analysis.

3) Scientists can detect living things or <u>evidence</u> of them, such as <u>fossils</u> or <u>remains</u>, in the samples. This 'fossil' is from Mars, though no one really seems sure *what* it is.

4) OK, so finding a couple of bacteria is a bit boring but that's how we started out on Earth...

3) Chemical Changes Show there's Life

1) Scientists are looking for <u>chemical changes</u> in the atmospheres of other <u>planets</u> and <u>moons</u> in our <u>solar system</u>.

2) They look at the planet's atmospheres from Earth — no spacecraft required.

3) Some changes are just caused by things like volcanoes but others are a <u>clue</u> that there's life there.

4) The amounts of <u>oxygen</u> and <u>carbon dioxide</u> in the Earth's atmosphere have <u>changed</u> over time — it's <u>very different</u> from what it'd be like if there was <u>no life</u> here. Plants have made oxygen levels <u>go up</u> but carbon dioxide levels <u>go down</u>. It's this kind of change that scientists look for on <u>other planets</u>.

4) The Right Conditions are needed for Life to Exist

1) For <u>life as we know it</u> to exist on other planets, <u>water</u> must be present.

2) This water must be in <u>liquid form</u> — ice or steam just won't do.

3) The planet must also have a <u>suitable atmosphere</u> — one which <u>protects</u> life from the harmful effects of <u>UV radiation</u>.

4) Another requirement is that the <u>atmospheric pressure</u> and <u>temperature</u> are not too <u>extreme</u>. Life can't <u>survive</u> if it's too cold, and if it's too hot then <u>DNA molecules</u> simply can't exist.

I've got SETI — it's great for watching telly on...

You need to learn the different ways that scientists are looking for life on other planets, and what the necessary conditions for <u>life</u> are. Cover the page and write notes about <u>how</u> the methods work and <u>what</u> they've found. And if you get any of it wrong, do it <u>again</u>.

The Three Types of Radiation

Some substances are radioactive. The nucleus of a radioactive atom is unstable.
It can break up and in the process give out nuclear radiation.

Nuclear Radiation: Alpha, Beta and Gamma (α, β and γ)

You need to remember three things about each type of radiation:
1) What they actually are.
2) How well they penetrate materials.
3) How strongly they ionise that material (ie. bash into atoms and knock electrons off).
   There's a pattern: The further the radiation can penetrate before hitting an atom and getting stopped, the less damage it will do along the way and so the less ionising it is.

Alpha Particles are Helium Nuclei ^4_2He

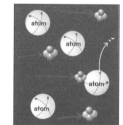

1) They are relatively big and heavy and slow moving.
2) They therefore don't penetrate into materials but are stopped quickly.
3) Because of their size they are strongly ionising, which just means
   they bash into a lot of atoms and knock electrons off them before
   they slow down, which creates lots of ions — hence the term 'ionising'.

Beta Particles are Electrons $^0_{-1}e$

1) These are between alpha and gamma in terms of their properties.
2) They move quite fast and they are quite small (they're electrons).
3) They penetrate moderately before colliding.
4) They are moderately ionising too. They ionise atoms by smashing into
   other electrons and knocking them away.
5) When a nucleus emits a β–particle, one of its neutrons turns to a proton.

Gamma Rays are Very Short Wavelength EM Waves

1) After an alpha or beta emission the nucleus sometimes has extra energy to get
   rid of. It does this by emitting a gamma ray.
2) Their properties are the opposite of alpha particle properties in a way.
3) They penetrate a long way into materials without being stopped.
4) This means they are weakly ionising because they tend to pass through rather
   than collide with atoms. Eventually they hit something and do damage.
5) A γ-ray has no mass and no charge.
6) Gamma emission never changes the proton
   or mass numbers of the nucleus.

A typical combined α– and γ– emission:

Remember What Blocks the Three Types of Radiation...

They really like this for Exam questions, so make sure you know what it takes to block each of the three:
Alpha particles are blocked by paper.
Beta particles are blocked by thin aluminium.
Gamma rays are blocked by thick lead.
Of course anything equivalent will also block them,
eg. skin will stop alpha, but not the others; a thin
sheet of any metal will stop beta; and very thick
concrete will stop gamma just like lead does.

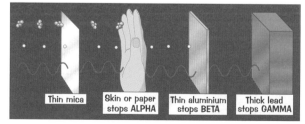

Thin mica | Skin or paper stops ALPHA | Thin aluminium stops BETA | Thick lead stops GAMMA

Learn the three types of radiation — it's easy as abc...

Alpha, beta and gamma. You do realise those are just the first three letters of the Greek
alphabet don't you: α, β, γ — just like a, b, c. They might sound like complex names to you but
they were just easy labels at the time. Anyway, learn all the facts about them — and scribble.

Background Radiation

Radioactivity is a <u>completely random</u> process — a bit like rolling a dice. You can <u>guess</u> when you'll next throw a 6, but you never <u>know for sure</u> (which is why casino owners are generally fairly wealthy). It's the <u>same</u> for nuclear decay — you never <u>know for sure</u> when a nucleus is going to spit something

Radioactivity is a Totally Random Process

<u>Unstable nuclei</u> will <u>decay</u> and in the process <u>give out radiation</u>. This process is entirely <u>random</u>. This means that if you have 1000 unstable nuclei, you can't say when <u>any one of them</u> is going to decay, and neither can you do anything at all <u>to make a decay happen</u>.

Each nucleus will just decay quite <u>spontaneously</u> in its <u>own good time</u>. It's completely unaffected by <u>physical</u> conditions like <u>temperature</u> or by any sort of <u>chemical bonding</u> etc.

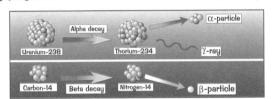

When the nucleus <u>does</u> decay it will <u>spit out</u> one or more of the three types of radiation, <u>alpha</u>, <u>beta</u> or <u>gamma</u>, and in the process the <u>nucleus</u> will often <u>change</u> into a <u>new element</u>.

Radioactivity is Measured in Becquerels, Bq

The <u>unit</u> used for measuring <u>radioactivity</u> is the <u>Becquerel</u> (Bq). <u>One Becquerel</u> is <u>one nucleus decaying per second</u>. So a count rate of <u>60 counts per minute (60 CPM)</u> would represent <u>1 Bq</u>.

Radioactivity is usually measured using a <u>Geiger-Muller tube</u> (or <u>G-M tube</u>, for short) together with a <u>counter</u>.

Background Radiation Comes From Many Sources

<u>Natural background radiation</u> comes from:

1) Radioactivity of naturally occurring <u>unstable isotopes</u> which are <u>all</u> around us — in <u>air</u>, in <u>food</u>, in <u>building materials</u> and in <u>rocks</u>.

2) Radiation from <u>space</u> — <u>cosmic rays</u>. These come mostly from the <u>Sun</u>.

3) Radiation due to <u>human activity</u> — ie. <u>fallout</u> from <u>nuclear explosions</u> or <u>dumped nuclear waste</u>. But this represents a <u>tiny</u> proportion of the total background radiation.

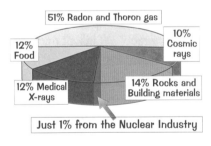

51% Radon and Thoron gas
10% Cosmic rays
12% Food
12% Medical X-rays
14% Rocks and Building materials
Just 1% from the Nuclear Industry

The Level of Background Radiation Changes Depending on Where You Are

1) At <u>high altitudes</u> (e.g. in <u>jet planes</u>) it <u>increases</u> because of more exposure to <u>cosmic rays</u>.

2) <u>Underground in mines</u>, etc. it increases because of the <u>rocks</u> all around.

3) Certain <u>underground rocks</u> can cause higher levels at the <u>surface</u>, especially if they release <u>radioactive radon gas</u>, which tends to get <u>trapped inside people's houses</u>. This varies widely across the UK depending on the <u>rock type</u>, as shown:

Millom

Coloured bits indicate more radiation from rocks

Background Radiation — it's no good burying your head in the sand...

Improve your background knowledge on the subject of radiation by learning all the facts on this page. Then when you think you've absorbed everything, write the four subheadings down on a piece of paper, and do a mini-essay under each heading. What could be more fun...

Uses of Radioactive Materials

1) Tracers in Medicine — always Short Half-life γ-emitters

1) Certain radioactive isotopes can be injected into people (or they can just swallow them) and their progress around the body can be followed using an external detector. A computer converts the reading to a TV display showing where the strongest reading is coming from.

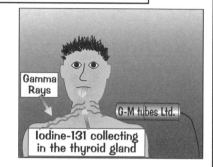

Gamma Rays

G-M tubes Ltd.

Iodine-131 collecting in the thyroid gland

2) A well known example is the use of Iodine-131 which is absorbed by the thyroid gland, just like normal Iodine-127, but it gives out radiation which can be detected to indicate whether or not the thyroid gland is taking in the iodine as it should.

3) All isotopes which are taken into the body must be gamma or beta emitters (never alpha), so that the radiation passes out of the body, and they should only last a few hours, so that the radioactivity inside the patient quickly disappears (ie. they should have a short half-life).

2) Tracers in Industry — For Finding Leaks

G-M tubes Ltd.

This is much the same technique as the medical tracers.
1) Radio-isotopes can be used to detect leaks in pipes.
2) You just squirt it in, and then go along the outside of the pipe with a detector to find areas of extra high radioactivity, which indicates the stuff is leaking out. This is really useful for concealed or underground pipes, to save you digging up half the road trying to find the leak.
3) The isotope used must be a gamma emitter, so that the radiation can be detected even through metal or earth which may be surrounding the pipe. Alpha and beta rays wouldn't be much use because they are easily blocked by any surrounding material.
4) It should also have a short half-life so as not to cause a hazard if it collects somewhere.

3) Sterilisation of Food and Surgical Instruments Using γ-Rays

1) Food can be exposed to a high dose of gamma rays which will kill all microbes thus keeping the food fresh for longer.

2) Medical instruments can be sterilised in just the same way, rather than boiling them.

3) The great advantage of irradiation over boiling is that it doesn't involve high temperatures so things like fresh apples or plastic instruments can be totally sterilised without damaging them.

unsterilised   Gamma source   sterilised

4) The food is not radioactive afterwards, so it's perfectly safe to eat.

5) The isotope used for this needs to be a very strong emitter of gamma rays with a reasonably long half-life (at least several months) so that it doesn't need replacing too often.

4) Radiotherapy — the Treatment of Cancer Using γ-Rays

1) Since high doses of gamma rays will kill all living cells, they can be used to treat cancers.
2) The gamma rays have to be directed carefully and at just the right dosage so as to kill the cancer cells without damaging too many normal cells.
3) However, a fair bit of damage is inevitably done to normal cells which makes the patient feel very ill. But if the cancer is successfully killed off in the end, then it's worth it.

5) Smoke detectors

1) A weak radioactive source is placed in the detector, close to two electrodes.
2) The source causes ionisation, and a current flows.
3) If there is a fire then smoke will absorb the radiation — the current stops and the alarm sounds.

Uses of Radioactive Materials

6) Thickness Control in Industry and Manufacturing

This is a classic application and is pretty popular in Exams. It's really very simple.

1) You have a radioactive source and you direct it through the stuff being made, usually a continuous sheet of paper or cardboard or metal etc.

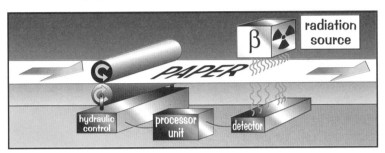

2) The detector is on the other side and is connected to a control unit.

3) When the amount of radiation detected goes down, it means the stuff is coming out too thick and so the control unit pinches the rollers up a bit to make it thinner again.

4) If the reading goes up, it means it's too thin, so the control unit opens the rollers out a bit. It's all clever stuff, but the most important thing, as usual, is the choice of isotope.

5) Firstly, it must have a long half-life (several years at least!), otherwise the strength would gradually decline and the control unit would keep pinching up the rollers trying to compensate.

6) Secondly, the source must be a beta source for paper and cardboard, or a gamma source for metal sheets. This is because the stuff being made must partly block the radiation.
If it all goes through, (or none of it does), then the reading won't change at all as the thickness changes. Alpha particles are no use for this since they would all be stopped.

7) Radioactive Dating of Rocks and Archaeological Specimens

1) The discovery of radioactivity and the idea of half-life gave scientists their first opportunity to accurately work out the age of rocks and fossils and archaeological specimens.

2) By measuring the amount of a radioactive isotope left in a sample, and knowing its half-life, you can work out how long the thing has been around. (See P. 103)

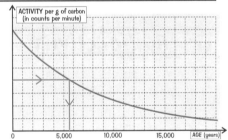

3) Igneous rocks contain radioactive uranium which has a ridiculously long half-life. It eventually decays to become stable isotopes of lead so the big clue to a rock sample's age is the relative proportions or ratio of uranium and lead isotopes.

4) Igneous rock also contains radioisotope potassium–40. Its decay produces stable argon gas and sometimes this gets trapped in the rock. Then it's the same process again — finding the relative proportions of potassium–40 and argon to work out the age.

8) Generating Power from Nuclear Fuel (Uranium)

1) Radioactive decay always gives out energy in the form of heat.

2) The radioactive decay inside the Earth is responsible for much of the heat down there.

3) By purifying uranium, we can set up a chain reaction where each decay causes another one. In this way we can increase the rate of reaction to generate lots of heat and then use it to produce electricity. This is what a nuclear power station does.

Will any of that be in your Exam? — isotope so...

First learn the eight headings till you can write them down from memory. Then start learning all the details that go with each one of them. As usual, the best way to check what you know is to do a mini-essay for each section. Then check back and see what details you missed. Nice.

Nuclear Radiation

Nuclear radiation has its uses, that's for sure, but it's not all good news.

Radiation Harms Living Cells

1) <u>Alpha</u>, <u>beta</u> and <u>gamma</u> radiation enter living cells and <u>collide</u> with molecules.

2) These collisions cause <u>ionisation</u>, which <u>damages</u> or <u>destroys</u> the molecules.

3) <u>Lower</u> doses tend to cause <u>minor</u> damage without <u>killing</u> the cell.

4) This can give rise to <u>mutant</u> cells which divide <u>uncontrollably</u>. This is <u>cancer</u>.

5) <u>Higher</u> doses tend to <u>kill cells</u> completely, which causes <u>radiation sickness</u> if a lot of your body cells all get <u>blatted at once</u>.

6) The <u>extent</u> of the harmful effects depends on <u>two</u> things:
   a) How much <u>exposure</u> you have to the radiation.
   b) The <u>energy</u> and <u>penetration</u> of the radiation emitted, since some types are more <u>hazardous</u> than others, of course.

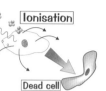

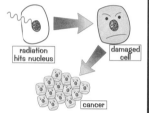

Outside The Body, β – and γ-Sources are the Most Dangerous

This is because <u>beta and gamma</u> can get <u>inside</u> to the delicate <u>organs</u>, whereas alpha is much less dangerous because it <u>can't penetrate the skin</u>.

Inside The Body, an α-Source is the Most Dangerous

<u>Inside the body</u> alpha-sources do all their damage in a <u>very localised area</u>. Beta and gamma sources on the other hand are <u>less dangerous</u> inside the body because they mostly <u>pass straight out</u> without doing much damage.

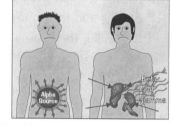

α, β and γ are Ionising Radiation

Ionisation is when an atom either <u>loses</u> or <u>gains</u> an <u>electron</u>. Simple as that — just don't forget it.

The Radioactivity of a Sample Always Decreases Over Time

1) This is <u>pretty obvious</u> when you think about it. Each time a <u>decay</u> happens and an alpha, beta or gamma is given out, it means one more <u>radioactive nucleus</u> has <u>disappeared</u>.

2) Obviously, as the <u>unstable nuclei</u> all steadily disappear, the <u>activity as a whole</u> will also <u>decrease</u>. So the <u>older</u> a sample becomes, the <u>less radiation</u> it will emit.

3) <u>How quickly</u> the activity <u>drops off</u> varies a lot. For <u>some</u> it takes <u>just a few hours</u> before nearly all the unstable nuclei have <u>decayed</u>, whilst others last for <u>millions of years</u>.

4) The problem with trying to <u>measure</u> this is that <u>the activity never reaches zero</u>, which is why we have to use the idea of <u>half-life</u> to measure how quickly the activity <u>drops off</u>.

5) Learn this <u>important definition</u> of <u>half-life</u>:
   Another definition of half-life is:
   "<u>The time taken for the activity (or count rate) to fall by half</u>". Use either.

   > **HALF-LIFE** is the **TIME TAKEN** for **HALF** of the radioactive atoms now present to **DECAY**

6) A <u>short half-life</u> means the <u>activity falls quickly</u>, because <u>lots</u> of the nuclei decay <u>quickly</u>.

7) A <u>long half-life</u> means the activity <u>falls more slowly</u> because <u>most</u> of the nuclei don't decay <u>for a long time</u> — they just sit there, <u>basically unstable</u>, but kind of <u>biding their time</u>.

Radiation Sickness — well, yes, it does all get a bit tedious...

This page is positively bristling with simple straightforward facts about radiation. Learn all these and you'll wonder how you ever managed to get by before. Three tiny little <u>mini-essays</u> practised two or three times and all this knowledge will be yours — forever. Enjoy.

Half-life Calculations: Step by Step

Measuring The Half-life of a Sample Using a Graph

1) This can <u>only be done</u> by taking <u>several readings</u> of <u>count rate</u> using a <u>G-M tube and counter</u>.
2) The results can then be <u>plotted</u> as a <u>graph</u>, which will <u>always</u> be shaped like the one below.
3) The <u>half-life</u> is found from the graph, by finding the <u>time interval</u> on the <u>bottom axis</u> corresponding to a <u>halving</u> of the <u>activity</u> on the <u>vertical axis</u>. Easy peasy really.

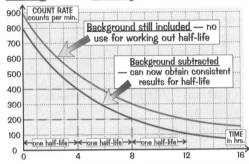

<u>One trick</u> you need to know is about the <u>background radiation</u>, which also enters the G-M tube and gives <u>false readings</u>. Measure the background count <u>first</u> and then <u>subtract it</u> from <u>every reading</u> you get, before plotting the results on the <u>graph</u>. Realistically, the <u>only</u> <u>difficult bit</u> is actually <u>remembering</u> about that for your <u>Exam</u>, should they ask you about it. They could also test that idea in a <u>calculation question</u>.

Do Half-Life Questions Step By Step

Half-life is maybe a little confusing, but Exam calculations are <u>straightforward</u> so long as you do them slowly, <u>STEP BY STEP</u>. Like this one:

<u>A VERY SIMPLE EXAMPLE:</u> The activity of a radio-isotope is 640cpm (counts per minute). Two hours later it has fallen to 40 cpm. Find the half life of the sample.

<u>ANSWER:</u> You must go through it in <u>short simple steps</u> like this:

<u>INITIAL</u> <u>count:</u>	(÷2)→	<u>after ONE</u> <u>half-life:</u>	(÷2)→	<u>after TWO</u> <u>half-lives:</u>	(÷2)→	<u>after THREE</u> <u>half-lives:</u>	(÷2)→	<u>after FOUR</u> <u>half-lives:</u>
640		320		160		80		40

Notice the careful <u>step by step method</u>, which tells us it takes <u>four half-lives</u> for the activity to fall from 640 to 40. Hence <u>two hours</u> represents four half-lives so the <u>half-life is 30 minutes</u>.

Relative Proportions Calculations — Easy, As Long As You Learn It

<u>Uranium isotopes</u> have a <u>very long half-life</u> and decay via a <u>series</u> of short-lived particles to produce <u>stable isotopes of lead</u>. The <u>relative proportions</u> of uranium and lead isotopes in a sample of <u>igneous rock</u> can therefore be used to <u>date</u> the rock, using the <u>known half-life</u> of the Uranium. It's as simple as this:

Initially	After one half-life	After two half-lives	After three half-lives
100% Uranium	50% Uranium	25% Uranium	12.5% Uranium
0% lead	50% lead	75% lead	87.5% lead

Ratio of Uranium to lead: (half-life of Uranium-238 = 4.5 billion years)

<u>Initially</u>	After <u>one half-life</u>	After <u>two half-lives</u>	After <u>three half-lives</u>
1:0	1:1	1:3	1:7

Similarly, the proportions of <u>potassium-40</u> and its stable decay product <u>argon-40</u> can also be used to <u>date igneous rocks</u>, so long as the <u>argon gas</u> hasn't been able to <u>escape</u>. The <u>relative proportions</u> will be exactly the <u>same</u> as for the uranium and lead example above. <u>Learn these ratios</u>:

Initially	After one half-life	After two half-lives	After three half-lives
100% : 0%	50% : 50%	25% : 75%	12.5% : 87.5%
1:0	1:1	1:3	1:7

Learn about Half-life — and get things in proportion...

These half-life calculations are really pretty simple. Try these:
1) An isotope has a half-life of 12 mins. How long will it take to drop from 840cpm to 210cpm?
2) A sample of rock contains uranium and lead in the ratio 75:525. How old is the rock?

Revision Summary for Module PD6

The Universe is completely mindblowing in its own right. But surely the most mindblowing thing of all is the very fact that we are actually here, sitting and contemplating the truly outrageous improbability of our own existence. If your mind isn't blowing, then it hasn't sunk in yet. Think about it. 15 billion years ago there was a huge explosion, but there was no need for the whole chain of events to happen which allowed (or caused?) intelligent life to evolve and develop to the point where it became conscious of its own existence, not to mention the very disturbing unlikelihood of it all. But we have. We're here. Maaaan — is that freaky or what? The Universe could so easily have existed without conscious life ever evolving. Or come to that, the Universe needn't exist at all. Just black nothingness. So why does life exist? And why are we here... ? Beats me — but stop dreaming and just get on with your lovely questions.

1) Calculate the speed of a tennis ball that travels 50 metres in 2 seconds.
2) If it accelerates to this speed from being stationary in 0.1 s, what is its acceleration?
3) Write down the Second Law of Motion. Illustrate with a diagram. What's the formula for it?
4) Explain what reaction force is. Is it important to know about it?
5) Explain the difference between mass and weight. What units are they measured in?
6) What is "terminal velocity"? Is it the same thing as maximum speed?
7) List the eleven parts of the Solar System starting with the Sun, and get them in the right order.
8) What's the difference between planets and stars?
9) What force keeps planets and satellites in their orbits? What shape are their orbits?
10) What is the famous 'inverse square' relationship all about? Sketch a diagram to explain it.
11) Sketch a diagram to explain the phases of the moon.
12) What and where are asteroids? What and where are meteorites? Is there a difference?
13) What and where are comets? What are they made of? Sketch a diagram of a comet orbit.
14) List the following in terms of relative size, starting with the smallest:
    Planets, Galaxies, Stars, Comets, Meteorites, Black Holes.
15) What is the Milky Way? Sketch it and show our Sun in relation to it.
16) Why would a black hole form? Why's it called 'black'? How can you spot one?
17) What important evidence needs to be explained by a theory describing the origin of the Universe?
18) What is the most likely theory for the origin of the Universe?
19) What are the two possible futures for the Universe? What do these possible futures depend upon?
20) Describe the first stages of a star's formation. Where does the initial energy come from?
21) What process eventually starts inside the star to make it produce so much heat and light?
22) What is a 'main sequence' star? How long does it last? What happens after that?
23) What are the two final stages of a small star's life? What are the final stages of a big star's life?
24) What is meant by a 'second generation' star? How do we know our Sun is one?
25) What does SETI stand for? Why are they looking for narrow band signals?
26) What two things do robots on planets send back? Which places have they sent robots to?
27) Describe two ways that scientists look for life on a planet without sending a spacecraft there.
28) Describe in detail the nature and properties of the three types of radiation: α, β, and γ.
29) How do the three types compare in penetrating power and ionising power?
30) Describe in detail how radioactive isotopes are used in each of the following:
    a) tracers in medicine   b) tracers in industry   c) sterilisation   d) radioactive dating
    e) treating cancer   f) smoke detectors   g) thickness control   h) electricity generation
31) List three sources of background radiation. What are the units of radioactivity?
32) Give a proper definition of half-life. How long and how short can half-lives be?
33) Sketch a typical graph of activity against time. Show how the half-life can be found.
34) The activity of a radio-isotope is 800cpm. 3 hours later it has fallen to 12.5cpm.
    Find the half-life of the sample.

Answers **P.45 1)** $Fe_2O_3 + 3H_2 \rightarrow 2Fe + 3H_2O$ **2)** $6HCl + 2Al \rightarrow 2AlCl_3 + 3H_2$ **P.47 1)** 64, 39, 84, 56, 35.5 **2)** 40, 148, 270.5 **P.48 1)** $ZnCl_2$ **2)** CH_4 **P.49 1)** 21.4g **2)** 93g **P.57 1 a)** $CaCO_3(s) + 2HCl(aq) \rightarrow CaCl_2(aq) + H_2O(l) + CO_2(g)$ **b)** $Ca(s) + 2H_2O(l) \rightarrow Ca(OH)_2(aq) + H_2(g)$ **c)** $H_2SO_4(aq) + 2KOH(aq) \rightarrow K_2SO_4(aq) + 2H_2O(l)$ **d)** $Fe_2O_3(s) + 3H_2(g) \rightarrow 2Fe(s) + 3H_2O(g)$ **4) a)** 40 **b)** 108 **c)** 44 **d)** 84 **e)** 241.5 **f)** 81 **g)** 106 **h)** 58.5 **6) a)** Fe_2O_3 **b)** CaF_2 **c)** C_5H_{12} **d)** $MgSO_4$ **7) a)** 186.8g **b)** 80.3g **c)** 20.1g **P.78 9)** 5V **24) a)** 48V **b)** 25Ω **P.89 18)** 6420J **20)** 2kW **21)** 20631J **22)** 945.5W **23)** 20m/s **24)** 10% **P.103 1)** 24 minutes **2)** 13.5 billion years **P.104 1)** 25 m/s **2)** 250 m/s^2 **34)** 30 minutes

Index

Index

Index

Index